The "Big Lie" in My Healthcare Bill

....

Why I "DON'T" Owe
What My Insurer Fails To Pay

....

Frank Lobb

Lobb's Analytical Works, LLC
P. O. Box 242
Nottingham, PA 19362

Library of Congress copyright application June 12, 2023
Tracking Number 1-12665782531

ISBN 979-8-218-19394-2

"Your in-network doctor or hospital shall "NOT" bill you in the event your insurer does not pay for the care you receive." This is straight out of the contract that every in-network healthcare provider signs. So, how is it you've been told **"you are responsible for whatever your insurance fails to pay"**? - - - Fortunately, only the first is true. The second is the "Big Lie" the American Healthcare System is using to pick your pocket and mine. And, I defy anyone in the Healthcare System to prove otherwise.

We can differ on
how to fix healthcare,
but we can't let them
lie to us.

Healthcare Costs in The United States

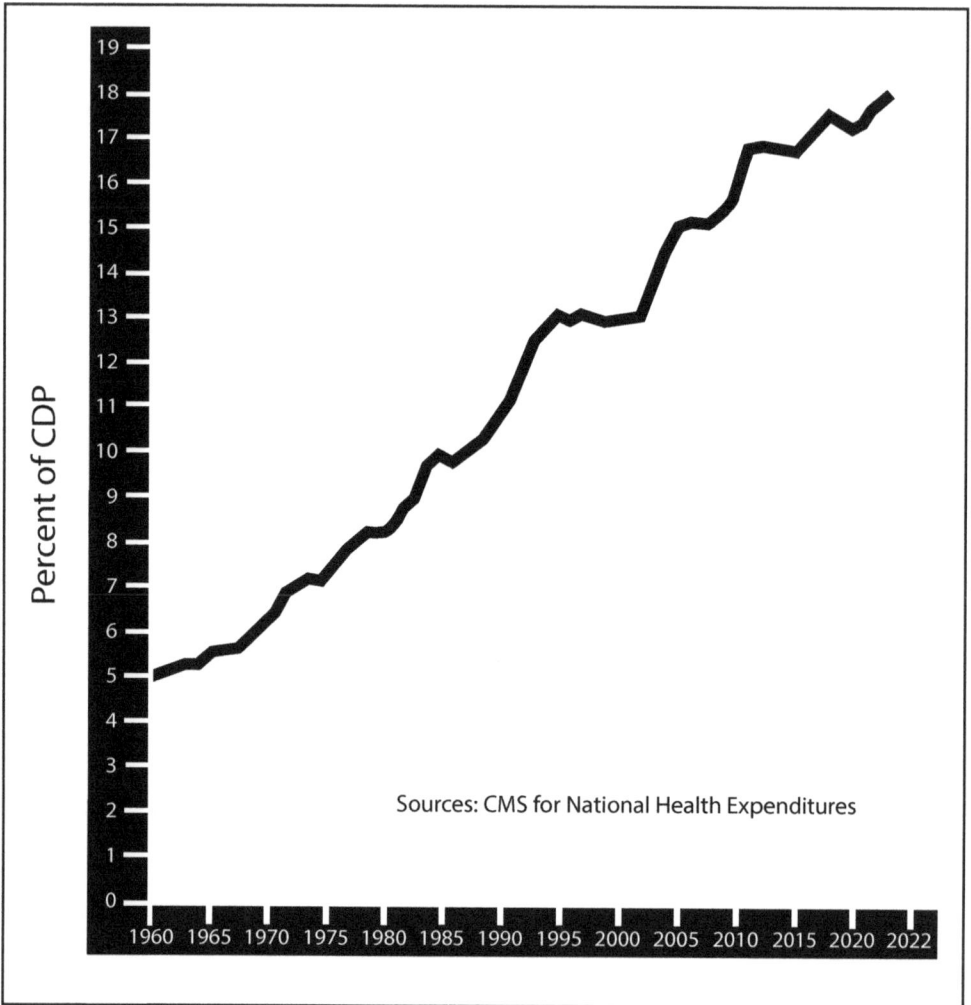

Percent of CDP

19
18
17
16
15
14
13
12
11
10
9
8
7
6
5
4
3
2
1
0

1960 1965 1970 1975 1980 1985 1990 1995 2000 2005 2010 2015 2020 2022

Sources: CMS for National Health Expenditures

Mission Statement

A recent study estimated 80% of the nation's healthcare bills are in error. Not that surprising when you consider there are some 77,000 different billing codes in the system and the participants can't agree on how they should be applied. Insurers opting to combine the care we receive into a single code to cut the cost of what they have to pay. While, the doctors, hospitals and other providers of healthcare services bill each and every code to create a larger and more profitable bill.

Providers billing every code in anticipation of an insurance company's underpayment. Insurance companies then underpaying and allowing the provider to pass what hasn't been paid onto you and me.

I hate to say it, but damn it's a beautiful scam!!! Everybody wins but us. The in-network provider gets to bill as much as they want. Our insurer gets to pay as little as they want. And, you and I get stuck for the difference, never to be told that we really don't owe what we are being billed. As the lead in the 1980s TV show The A-Team was fond of saying, *"It's a beautiful thing when a plan comes together."*

But, it gets worse. The in-network contract that allows an insurance company to underpay a bill goes so far as to allow "zero" payment, as in no payment at all. In which case, the provider will be looking to you or me to pay the entire bill. Even though the contract the provider has signed forbids passing any such unpaid amount on to you or me.

Therefore, the mission of the book is twofold:

Section ONE: To explain what we are ACTUALLY owed from our health insurance.

Section TWO: To provide the means of stopping an outrageous healthcare bill dead in its tracks.

A Word of Appreciation

II would like to thank the following individuals for sharing their insight and knowledge of the American Health Care System. While not all of these people were supportive of my efforts, every one of them contributed to the material in the book.

Joe Pitts	Retired U. S. Congressman & Chair of the House Subcommittee on Health
Dominic Pileggi	Pennsylvania State Senator
Edwin J. Feulner	Past President, the Heritage Foundation
Art Hershey	Retired Pennsylvania State Representative
Art Caplan	Nationally Acclaimed Bioethicist
Mary Agnes Carey	Kaiser Health News
Jerry Kritz	Retired Criminal Defense Attorney
Dr. David Frankel	University of Pennsylvania Hospital
Michael Cannon	Director Healthcare Programs, Cato Institute
Karl Stark	Philadelphia Inquire
Carl Witte	Retired Senior Hospital Administrator
Greg Heller	Attorney, Young, Ricchiuti, Caldwell & Heller
Andrew Schlafly	General Counsel, Association of American Physicians & Surgeons
David Senoff	Attorney; Caroselli, Beachier, McTierman & Conboy
Clark Neiley	Constitutional Attorney, Institute for Justice
Sam McMicheal	Attorney, McMicheal, Heiney & Sebastian
Joe Roda	Attorney, Roda & Nast
Valerie Gatesman	Attorney, U. S. Department of Labor
Twila Brawley	Director, Citizens Council for Health Freedom
Sue Blevins	Author of Cato Institute's Book, "Medicar's Midlife Crisis"
Dr. Fred Himmelstein	Emergency Physician; Jennersville Regional Hospital
Dr. Cecile Pileggi	Physician; Chester County, PA
Ken Woodward	Proofer and Supporter Extraordinaire

Plus a host of other doctors, nurses, health care professionals and interested individuals who shared their time and knowledge. --- **To all of you, a very a sincere Thank You!**

The "Big Lie" in My Healthcare Bill

Why I "DON'T" Owe
What My Insurer Fails To Pay

© 2023 Frank Lobb
ISBN 978-8-218-19394-2

Once again dedicated to the memory of Sandra Lobb and the loving support, of Angie Lobb

Table of Contents

Appendix

1. Typical Request for an Explanation of a Bill
2. Follow-up Letter One
3. Follow-up Letter Two
4. Follow-up Letter Three
5. A Typical Provider Agreement
6. NAIC's Suggested Enrollee Hold Harmless Requirement
7. A Typical State's Enrollee Hold Harmless Requirement
8. Medicare's ABN
9. Notes from 67 Pages of Terms & Conditions

"If you don't think healthcare is about power, you haven't been paying attention."

Don Berwick, MD
Former Administrator of the Centers for Medicare & Medicaid Services

Forward

Not that long ago my wife and I spent a night at a B&B in Harpers Ferry, West Virginia. In the morning, we shared breakfast with a married couple who just happened to both be physicians at a large metropolitan hospital. Because of my interest in healthcare, I had to ask a few questions while my wife kicked me under the table to pursue something other than healthcare over breakfast. Retracting my shins and pressing on, I asked, *"Given that the insurance industry's Provider Agreements allow hospitals to charge as much as they want, while allowing an insurance company to pay as little as they want, how badly is the patient getting stuck with the unpaid balance for the benefit of the hospital and the insurance company? How badly is the public being skewered – Just how big is the problem?"*

The two doctors looked at each other and broke out laughing. Not because my question was ridiculous, but because of how familiar they were with just how badly the public is being fleeced. The husband even quoted a study showing 46% of what hospitals are charging is being created by the billing process. In short, they made it abundantly clear that the problem is all-too-real and the public is being ripped-off big-time.

The following week I had an appointment with an orthopedic surgeon where the aid preparing me to see the doctor spoke of the amazing advances they were seeing in technology. I replied that it's a shame the cost of healthcare is exploding even faster. Where in the aid looked around to be sure he wouldn't be overheard, and then whispered, *"It really doesn't cost that much."*

I cite these two examples to set a tone and goal for the book, because, you and I are not about to change the American Healthcare System. Furthermore, no one on a white horse is going to come galloping over the hill to rescue us from a fraudulent healthcare bill. We are going to have to live with the healthcare system we have. And "live" is the operative word because we are talking about life itself. Unfortunately, the only choice we are being given is whether to allow ourselves to be counted among the sheep to be fleeced.

Introduction:

The most accepted part of paying a bill is our right to receive a bill we can understand. One where you or I can sit down, add up the charges and ensure the bill is correct. In fact, at the close of every month my wife religiously makes this journey through our family bills. And, while the accounting for the majority of the bills is spot-on, it certainly isn't true for every bill we get. Some are flat wrong or at least require some correction. We recently had dinner out to celebrate a rebate my wife won by challenging a large credit card bill. The bottom line is that all the bills we receive contain the information we need to understand them. And, if some additional information is needed to confirm the appropriateness or accuracy of a bill, we can get it by simply asking for it.

However, that certainly isn't true for the healthcare bills we receive. Here, we typically get a bill that only lists an unadjusted total cost, a reduced or adjusted cost after insurance, and then a total of what we are supposed owe. We are simply expected to accept on blind faith that the long list of individual charges that make up a significant healthcare bill, along with the various discounts our health insurance is supposed to provide, and the individual amounts of coverage we are owed have all been properly addressed and totaled. Simply put, we are expected to accept the bill as presented with no ability to check its appropriateness or accuracy. - - - This is a complete contradiction to both law and precedent in the United States. And, it's how the American Healthcare System picks our pocket while secretly rationing the healthcare we are allowed to receive.

Some Personal History

It took me ten years of suing the healthcare insurance industry to learn the details of the scheme the American Healthcare System uses to deny the care and coverage we both need and are owed. Care and coverage that would have saved the life of my wife Sandy. Care her doctor pleaded for. Care I demanded the right to pay for. And, care that was repeatedly refused.

While my ten years of litigation failed to get the justice I sought for Sandy, I was able to "drag" out of the insurance industry, piece by piece, exactly how they mislead the public. More specifically, how they were able to deny the care Sandy needed even though I was demanding to pay for it outside of any participation from our healthcare insurance company. In fact, the proof I obtained on how the System denies care and coverage was so damming, I just assumed Washington would act if shown the truth.

Boy was I naive. After countless phone calls, letters, meetings, speaking engagements, published articles and three books it has become very clear that I could not have been more wrong about Washington. For, while Democrats and Republicans may have different reasons for preserving the status quo, they are united when it comes to protecting the American Healthcare System. Consequently, I have lost all energy for righting the System. That battle for me is lost. I have run at that brick wall far too often only to come away shaken by our leaders' refusal to even discuss the misrepresentation and fraud in the American Healthcare System.

A recent experience demonstrates just how clearly the battle has been lost. I was asked by a very accomplished attorney and advocate for healthcare reform to participate in a conference call to discuss how healthcare insurance companies can retroactively deny coverage for care that has been pre-approved, rendered and covered. I quickly emailed back agreeing to participate. However, I made the mistake of including an explanation of the secret contracts that allow these reversals of coverage. I never heard another word about the conference call.

On one hand, the attorney was very comfortable publically criticizing the injustice of these retroactive denials of coverage. But, when given the opportunity to understand the misrepresentation and fraud used to create them, she was completely unwilling to discuss the issue. And, I can say unwilling because I tried repeatedly to reconnect and never got so-much as a thanks, but no thanks.

This wasn't my first similar experience with the legal community. A prominent Philadelphia attorney simply said *"This is above my paygrade"* and walked away. One of the largest law firms in the country made their departure as simple as *"We aren't saying you are wrong, just that we aren't interested in pursuing the matter."* And, there is the experience of having the Chair of the House Sub-Committee on Health of the U. S. Congress ask me why I should care if I was prevented from paying for Sandy's care.

If you can't get folks in the legal community or our politicians to even discuss the possibility of misrepresentation and fraud in the American Healthcare System, you and I need to conclude that the battle to right the American Healthcare System has been lost. And, <u>we have been left to fend for ourselves</u>.

PART ONE
---The How & Why of the Fraud

Chapter 1

....

*"Stand up to your obstacles and
do something about them. You will
find they haven't half the strength
you think they have"*
                    Norman Vincent Peale

Setting the Stage for Pushing Back
Our "New" Reality

It used to be said there are only two certainties in life — death and taxes. Today, we have the additional certainty of an outrageous healthcare bill that can take our savings, our home and everything we have ever hoped to have for ourselves and our family. And, in most cases, the only thing standing between us and this financial disaster is the hope that our health insurance will be there to pay the bills — bills we are all likely to face at some point in life.

In my father's time, operating a car required a detailed understanding of how it worked. Valves had to be set, changing a flat tire was a routine necessity, ignition points died and battery failure was ever-so common in winter. Today, we simply get in our car, turn the key and drive. It's that simple. However, the technology that makes our cars so simple and reliable to operate is well beyond the understanding of the average driver. Automatic braking, computer controlled engines, electronically driven transmissions, suspensions that adjust to the conditions of the road and batteries that last for years are beyond the understanding of the average driver. In short, the very complexity of today's automobile forces us to approach our cars as a turn-the-key and drive necessity.

Health insurance has gone through a similar evolution. The understandable health insurance that our parents enjoyed is no longer available. In its place is a product that defies understanding while placing our health and financial wellbeing at serious risk. For while the increase in the complexity of our automobiles brought simpler and more reliable operation, the evolution of health insurance has brought just the opposite. It has brought an ever-more complex system that we are asked to accept on blind faith.

Returning to my father's time, blind faith wasn't required when the family needed healthcare and coverage. We had an insurance broker named Tom Hoyle who represented us and was as much a family friend as he was our broker. A man we could count on to explain the system. A man who would always put our needs first. And, a man who would always get us the coverage we were owed. - - - That man no longer exists. The Tom Hoyles of my father's time are dead and gone. And, so too is any expectation of being able to understand the detailed workings of the American Healthcare System.

So, the book will not attempt to provide that detailed understanding. To use my automobile analogy, we are not about to disassemble the engine and transmission, or even go under the hood. Rather, the book is aimed solely at giving you the knowledge you need to push back against an improper and fraudulent healthcare bill. To, in essence, allow you to turn the key on your health insurance and drive, i.e., to put you in the driver's seat. In short, the book is aimed at allowing you to ignore the mind-blowing complexity and misrepresentation of today's healthcare system and simply turn the key on the "care and coverage" you and your family are "owed."

This is not to say that the majority of people with health insurance don't get the care they need and some level of coverage. Just the opposite. Most get the care their doctor prescribes and see the bill covered, just as long as the deductible has been met and we are willing to accept the System's "Big Lie." This is particularly true for routine trips to a doctor or treatments for minor healthcare problems. However, it's also true that we are seeing a dramatic shrinkage in the coverage we can expect as insurance companies modify their plans to include ever-greater deductibles and shrinking levels of coverage. Furthermore, insurers are becoming increasingly aggressive in denying coverage (rationing) for the expensive forms of healthcare and in pursuing an unpaid healthcare bill.

After all, just as anyone who has attended a course on sales or marketing will tell you, *"You go where the money is."* And, that is exactly what the insurance industry is doing. They are: 1.) Dramatically raising the cost of their plans, 2.) Dramatically raising the required deductible before a plan provides coverage, 3.) Aggressively rationing expensive care for chronic illnesses and end of life healthcare, and 4.) Pursuing unpaid healthcare bills.

You doubt me? The first two points are part of the everyday news cycle. And, the third point only requires a little looking. For example, my wife and I had dinner with a woman who has a PhD in care for the elderly, is employed as fulltime consultant for a large law firm, lectures across the country on the intersection of eldercare and the law, and who spent years as the head of a large nursing and rehabilitation facility. So, as part of our dinner discussion, I ran point #3 past her to see if she agreed with it. And, given that her expertise is in eldercare and the law, I framed the discussion around Medicare Advantage. Medicare Advantage being nothing more than the private plans that we get from our employer, but that the Government purchases as an alternative to Medicare. My friend's "immediate" response to my mentioning Medicare Advantage was, *"Oh, you mean the no care at all plan. Don't ever let yourself get talked in to one of those."*

Her response wasn't the intellectual response of one making a factual comparison of one plan versus another that I had expected. It was an emotional response driven by having had to personally deal with the rationing of healthcare by Medicare Advantage plans. Plans that promote membership by offering attractive additional benefits to a new retiree, and then rationing the expensive end-of-life care that becomes ever-more necessary as one approaches the end of life. Thus becoming my friend's *"no care at all plan"* when the option to switch back to Medicare and its assurance of care and coverage gets increasingly lost in the law and a particular time of the year in which to apply.

In 2021, Medicare Advantage plans refused 2-million pre-authorizations for healthcare that was requested for their elderly enrollees. Yet, the membership in these plans is growing and now exceeds the membership of Medicare. Furthermore, this growth is forecast to continue as insurers bombard retirees with never-ending commercials that only show healthy and vibrant Medicare Advantage retirees basking in the added benefits of a Medicare Advantage plan while completely ignoring the plight of the aged and infirmed enrollee fighting for life because of a *"no care at all plan."* When people age under a Medicare Advantage plan, they are *"likely to have more health problems"* (KFF, formally the Kaiser Family Foundation). *"The primary concern with Medicare Advantage plans is the quality of care they deliver when a member has serious health issues"* (David Lipschutz, Associate Director of the Center for Medicare Advocacy). And, Medicare Advantage patients *"too often find it more difficult to get the care they need"* (AARP, October 2023). All quotes demonstrating the flagrant rationing in the Medicare Advantage plans and our private healthcare insurance industry.

As to the question of why all this rationing, in 2021, the gross margin for Medicare Advantage plans was more than double what insurers got for the plans that they supplied through an employer.

It's my personal opinion that there just isn't a better example of where the American Healthcare System is headed than the private plans of Medicare Advantage. For, it is within these plans that insurers have the greatest freedom to ration care and coverage. After all, Government is paying for the plans, and the people most effected by the rationing are at the end of life where any claim of a denial of care or coverage will likely be lost in an individual's death or the U. S. Supreme Court's decision that rationing must be a fundamental part of any health insurance scheme. Medicare Advantage providing essentially an open road to the rationing that insurers have sought for more than thirty years, all the while hiding it by denying that any such rationing is even possible.

This is the reality of the rationing we face. Because, it's driven by the money and power of a 4-trillion dollar healthcare market that demands rationing be a fundamental part of the American Healthcare System. Rationing that can only exist through misrepresentation and dishonesty when it comes to the promises made to sell a plan, the care a provider actually delivers, and the System's adherence to the terms and conditions of a hidden Provider Agreement. And, at the very core of all this change and dishonesty is the American Healthcare System's "Big Lie." Because, it allows providers to bill you and me for what insurers are increasingly refusing to pay/cover.

"It is understood that you assume the financial responsibility of paying for all services rendered either through third-party payers (your insurance company) or being personally responsible for payment for any services which are not covered by your insurance policies."---

This is a direct quote from one of the largest and most prestigious healthcare providers in the country. Yet, it's a statement that can be <u>readily shown to be completely false on its face</u>. However, it needs to serve as a reality check for how the American Healthcare System plans to shift more and more of the cost of their rationing onto you and me by way of their "Big Lie."

An insurer can simply deny coverage and then sit back and allow the provider to go after you or me to pay what hasn't been covered – assuming we were able to get the rationed care in the first place.

The Issue at the "Core" of the Fraud

We've all had the experience of being asked to sign a form

that contains a statement similar to the one highlighted above. A form that the provider would have us believe is a binding contract to pay whatever our insurer fails to pay. Well, surprise, surprise! Both the agreement we sign and any bill we get for what hasn't been covered is rooted in fraud. That's because the contract (a Provider Agreement) that every in-network provider of healthcare has to sign to be in-network, requires the provider to: 1.) Provide all the care our doctor believes we need, 2.) Look only to the insurer for payment, and 3.) Refrain from billing us for any necessary healthcare that our insurer has refused to cover. Three requirements spelled out as clear as day in every one of the insurance industry's Provider Agreements.

However, as clear as these provisions are in these Provider Agreements, we are destined to lose an argument based on our right to receive free healthcare. After all, common sense dictates the very opposite. And, it will certainly be argued that we accepted responsibility for paying for the care when we agreed to receive it. Adding to the strength of that argument will be the fact that no one we will ever speak to will have read a Provider Agreement. Furthermore, your insurer isn't going to volunteer a copy of a Provider Agreement that they claim to be intellectual property and secret. Nor will the provider that sent a bill provide a copy as the Agreement specifically bars any such disclosure. However, just because no one will have seen one of these Agreements, or be willing to share one of them with us, doesn't mean they don't exist, or <u>aren't legally binding</u>. It just means the American Healthcare System has done an excellent job of hiding them to support the "Big Lie." Which would appear to leave you and me in the losing position of having to prove we don't have to pay a healthcare bill that our insurer has claimed falls outside the coverage of our plan. That is simply not where you and I want to be if dragged into court for an unpaid healthcare bill.

Fortunately, there is a game-changer readily available to us. It's called the Federal Fair Debt Collection Practices Act (FDCPA). The Act gives us the right to demand an understandable explanation for any bill we wish to challenge. And, because healthcare bills have been shown to contain an unreasonable number of errors, the U. S. Consumer Financial Protection

Bureau (here after the CFPB) has ruled that those engaged in the collection of a healthcare bill *"must conduct reasonable and timely investigations of consumer disputes to verify the accuracy"* of any purported healthcare debt. Consequently, all we have to do is ask a few questions in a timely manner and we can completely reverse the burden of proof for a healthcare bill. In essence, by simply following the recommendations of the CFPB, and requesting the requirements of the FDCPA, we can put the in-network provider or bill collector in the position of either abandoning our bill or having to disclose the misrepresentation and fraud that is at the heart of the American Healthcare System and its "Big Lie."

Rather than our having to prove we shouldn't be made to pay a bill that our health insurance has failed to pay, we can put the provider, our insurer, any collection agency, and the entire American Healthcare System in the position of having to prove they have the right to bill us under the very explicit terms of their hidden Provider Agreements. Terms the System isn't allowed to even discuss, let alone disclose to a court in a collection process.

However, the situation gets even better if the provider actually sends our bill to a collection agency. Because, our bill will very likely have been bundled with a number of other unpaid bills and then sold as a group to the collection agency. It's an outcome we should almost celebrate rather than dread. Because in selling our bill, the provider will have "SEVERED" their ability to provide the very information the FDCPA and the CFPB call for to have a bill ruled accurate and enforceable.

All a collection agency can receive when it purchase an unpaid healthcare bill is the bill itself or the bare debt. Nothing else, regardless of whether it has been bundled or sold separately. The assumption being, that the bill is enforceable on its face. Therefore, no supporting information is needed, i.e., none of the information that the FDCPA and the CFPB allow us to require for bill to be viewed as enforceable. In fact, the Health Insurance Portability & Accountability Act (HIPAA), bars a provider from supplying the very information needed to demonstrate the accuracy of a bill. So, unless Congress rewrites HIPAA, and insurers rewrite their Provider Agreements, a collection agency will be barred from receiving the very information that the FDCPA and the CFPB would require for a bill to be viewed as enforceable. We just have to be smart enough to properly request this information within 30 days of receiving a bill.

Stating this as simply as I can. The American Healthcare Billing System is built on **the belief that you and I are just not SMART enough to properly question a bill within 30 days of receiving it,** a failure that allows the collection "process" to **AUTOMATICALLY** declare a bill accurate on its face and demand payment in full. Case closed! The only issue left to be determined by a court or the collection process is how and when we will be forced to pay it.

Yes, you and I can argue that we have made countless phone calls to our insurer to contest the coverage of a bill. And, we can argue that we've written countless letters disputing the amount of a bill. However, unless we have asked the right questions, done it in writing and done it within 30 days of receiving the bill from a collection agency, all the issues surrounding a bill will be dead as far as a court and the American Healthcare Billing System are concerned. Our bill will be effectively cast in hard and immovable concrete.

A point of confusion that can easily arise over the enforceability of a healthcare bill, is the ability to negotiate a lower payment on a bill. It's an ability that has nothing to do with whether a bill is accurate or enforceable. It's simply the likelihood that a billing office or collection agency will readily agree to accept a lower payment in exchange for a promise to pay. In fact, it happens all the time with discounts in the range of 20 percent or more, and payments stretched out over some protracted period of time. However, the ability to negotiate a reduced bill, or payments over time, should not be confused with contesting the enforceability of a bill through the requirements of the FDCPA and the recommendations of the CFPB. Furthermore, the book argues the issue of a bill should always be one of whether an in-network provider can even show it has a right to bill us, and certainly whether they can adequately demonstrate the accuracy of a bill. These are two well supported issues, because CFPB has shown that upwards of 80 percent of all healthcare bills are in error. They are also two issues that can cause a provider or bill collector to fall flat on their face when it comes to enforcing a bill under the requirements of the FDCPA and the recommendations of the CFPB.

The bottom line is that so long as we dispute a bill by asking a few simple questions within 30 days of receiving a bill, we can effectively strip the American Healthcare System of its approach to enforcing an in-network healthcare bill. And, all we will have done is ask a few simple questions.

The best example I can think of to illustrate the fix that the FDCPA, together with the actions of the CFPB, can put an in-network provider or collection agency attempting to enforce a healthcare bill is to liken health insurance to a house built in the 1920s. Both were built well in the past and then painted over year after year to hide the growing structural problems. However, the real estate market recognized the problem and instituted laws that require the owner of a 1920s house to strip away the paint and disclose the actual structure of the house before it can be sold. Unfortunately, Congress and the American Healthcare System have had no such attack of conscience. Our healthcare System and laws still allow insurance companies to sell their plans with all their many coats of glossy paint remaining in place to obscure the underlying structure of a plan and the System's "Big Lie." However, <u>Federal Law governing the enforcement of a healthcare bill can be used to strip away all that paint. If, we are just smart enough to ask for the paint to be stripped away</u>.

In Summary:
The only binding agreement on who owes what on in-network healthcare is your insurer's Provider Agreement. And, it states:
    1.) We are to get all the healthcare "OUR" doctor says we need.

and

    2.) We can "NOT" be billed if our insurer fails to pay for it. <u>Consequently</u>, an in-network provider can be

made to "PROVE" it has the right to bill us when coverage is denied for the healthcare our doctor says we need.

However, there is nothing in this book, or anything I can say or do to guarantee you won't be pursued in court to pay an unjust in-network healthcare bill. This is particularly true for a large bill that can be viewed as justifying the cost of litigation. What the book can do is provide you with the information that the American Healthcare System needs to keep secret and the FDCPA, along with the CFPB, require be disclosed. And, in so doing, give you the ability to shift the burden of proof on a healthcare bill away from you and onto whoever is pursuing payment, i.e., to require the provider or collection agency to prove it has a right to bill you rather than you having to prove the bill is inaccurate or unenforceable. Most importantly, it's a shift that carries with it the clear message that proceeding with the enforcement of the bill will risk exposing the entirety of the American Healthcare System's "Big Lie."

Put in the simplest English I know. I can teach you how to fight an improper healthcare bill, as I have done for myself and my family. What I can't do is keep the fight from coming to your door.

This is a hugely important point, because nothing is more critical in a court fight than the ability to pay for the cost of the litigation. I can say this from very personal experience. I was in court for eight years against one of the largest healthcare insurance companies in the country and had no choice but to represent myself throughout those eight years – because I couldn't afford to do otherwise. The insurer, on the other hand, suffered no such problem and generated motion after motion that would have bankrupted me if I hadn't been acting as my own attorney. That said, even here the insurer was able to literally run out the clock, never once showing any concern for the cost of the litigation, or the time and effort consumed by the case.

The point being, that once a provider or collection agency decides it's worth pursuing a bill, and actually files a complaint in court seeking payment, you will only have two options. One, you can choose to pursue some form of settlement where you agree to pay at least a portion of the bill. Or, you can litigate the bill through an attorney and join the fight. Making sure your attorney is familiar with the material in the book and is willing to take on the "Big Lie." However, having spent 8 years in court fighting the System, I can't recommend this as a road you want to even consider going down.

There is one possible exception to what I just said, if you can find an attorney willing to test the water without committing to an all-out fight. You can have the attorney file a reply requesting the information the book recommends and see what happens. There is always the possibility that whoever has filed the complaint will reconsider the risk of going forward and simply withdraw the complaint. However, if the decision is made to cobble some form of a reply and move forward with enforcing the bill, you will most likely be well advised to dismiss your attorney and seek some form of negotiated settlement. Because the other side will have committed to the cost of the litigation needed to enforce the bill. And, even more importantly, they will have committed to bring all guns to bear in defending the System's "Big Lie." In essence, you will be taking on the entire American Healthcare System.

Of course, there is always an additional option. But, certainly not a good one! You can choose to simply ignore a bill. And then just hope it goes away. Unfortunately, that is not how the system works. In fact, this last option is exactly what the System is counting on to simplify their collection process. Because, if you or your attorney isn't ready to show up in court to contest a bill, the court is not only free to hand down a judgement ordering you to pay the full amount of the bill, but effectively legally bound to do exactly that.

My father once accused me of having too many fights in my life. I pushed back hard saying that fights are largely things that find us. So, the real measure of who we are is how we stand up to the fights that find us.

The FDCPA, along with the actions of the CFPB, can provide you and me with a means of standing up against a system designed to pick our pocket, and push far too many families into bankruptcy. However, neither the FDCPA, nor the CFPB, is a silver bullet. They simply provide you and me with a means of forcing whoever sent us a bill to step back and consider whether the financial reward for pursuing a bill is worth the risk of having to publically disclose the System's inability to provide the information the FDCPA and the CFPB call for.

All this is to simply say that the American Court System doesn't guarantee justice. It simply provides a stage upon which we can fight for it.

There is an additional example I just have to add, if not for any particular clarity it brings to what I am suggesting for a healthcare bill, but at least for the humor it adds to the subject.

My good friend the retired defense attorney was recently cited for smoking on the beach and threatened with arrest. He calmly informed the officer that the town's jurisdiction ends at the high-water mark on the beach, and that both his chair and cigar were beyond the high-water mark as they have been for the past 40 years. Consequently, the issue was no longer Jerry's cigar, but rather the threat he presented to the town's ability to restrict smoking along the entire beach. Therefore, Jerry's problem simply vanished as he sat back down to enjoy his cigar.

An Even "Larger" Issue

The ability to pick our pocket with a fraudulent healthcare bill is only the most obvious part of the "Big Lie" and the American Healthcare System's scheme to ration healthcare. An even bigger, but less obvious issue, is the insurance industry's ability to change plans without providing any notice, review or meaningful disclosure.

Every year my wife and I sit down with the healthcare insurance broker that we have used over many years to provide health insurance for the employees in our family business. This year was no exception. The broker laid out the eight or so plans that would be available for the coming year. Each significantly different in cost and coverage from last year's plan. And, none easily comparable to the other seven, much less the plan we had for the past year. That's right, all were completely new plans with different costs and coverages laid out in a matrix that can literally blow your mind.

So I asked the broker, for the first time in our long history, how is all this change possible. How can an insurer make so many changes without altering a pile of contracts? I reminded him that we know insurers have to be supported by contracts. So, how can an insurer make all these changes without making comparable contract changes?

The broker leaned back in his chair, and for the first time appeared to recognize the significance of what I was saying. In fact, he laughed through his *"it just can't be. There can't be new or revised contracts to support all these new plans."*

But, I reminded him that there has to be a contract someplace, because the laws of every state require a state approved contract (Provider Agreement) between an insurer and every one of their in-network providers of healthcare. So, how can that contract be changed and approved every year to accommodate all the new and revised plans?

A light once again sparked to life on the broker's face. ***"There can only be one contract, because the task of creating one for every new plan is simply beyond the ability of the system."*** I then replied, *"Case made and closed."*

The biggest feature of the American Healthcare System's "Big Lie" is the insurance industry's ability to pay as little as an insurer wants, whenever it wants. Which every healthcare insurance company is guaranteed under the terms of its state approved Provider Agreements. Which, in turn, translates to insurers being able to change their plans at-will because they already have a blanket right to deny coverage whenever they choose. In essence, to go from 80 percent to 70 percent coverage in a revised plan simply falls under an insurer's right to pay as little as they want. And, the "Big Lie" makes the change work, because, it allows the provider to pass the cost of what isn't being covered onto you and me.

Yes, the "Big Lie" dramatically simplifies enforcement of the American Healthcare System's fraudulent bills. But, more importantly, the "Big Lie" allows healthcare insurance companies to cut coverage and raise the cost for their plans without ever having to submit them for review or provide the public with an <u>understandable</u> explanation of the changes.

The "Magnitude" of the Problem

The average individual in the United States will spend somewhere between $300,000 and $400,000 on healthcare over his or her lifetime in today's dollars and more than 100 million Americans are currently burdened with unpaid medical debt. Now, add to that the $433.2 billion per year in out of pocket expenses that we are paying for healthcare and the scope of our problem begins to take shape. Compound all that expense out over a lifetime at say 2.5 percent annually (the Federal Reserve's targeted rate of inflation) and the numbers get even larger.

Add to these mind-blowing costs the fact that, even today, the primary cause of family bankruptcy in the U. S. is an unpaid healthcare bill. And, on top of that, we need to add in the fact that a person born today is expected to live to be roughly 103 years old. Which can only make the problem worse for our nation's children when the average family today can't deal with an unexpected $400 bill.

The inescapable conclusion is that each of us need reliable health insurance to have any hope of affording the healthcare we are likely to need over our lifetime. It's analogous to having house insurance or automobile insurance. If tragedy strikes, we can't afford to lose the cost of our home to a fire, or the loss of our automobile in an accident. These losses are just too great to absorb without irreparably changing one's life. However, there is at least a reasonable likelihood that our house won't burn down, or our car won't be destroyed in an accident. Unfortunately, we can't say that for healthcare. With healthcare we know we are going to face $300,000 to $400,000 in healthcare costs and quite possibly a great deal more. The only question is how we are going to pay for it. In fact, it's almost a certainty that we will be subjected to far higher costs as all the forecasts on healthcare suggest. Unless, of course, we end-run the system by dying early. Then we can simply have the healthcare costs leading up to our death classified as an uncollectable debt. Unless, we have savings, a home or a family, because then whatever healthcare costs we leave behind will be pursued even in death. In fact, the law allows courts to go back seven years to void a financial transaction (say the sale or gift of a house to a child or relative) to satisfy an unpaid healthcare bill. It's another of the realities we have to face.

Fortunately, most of us have some form of health insurance. And, if we live to be 65 years of age, we can be assured of receiving Medicare to cover much of the cost of our healthcare. However, prior to reaching 65, those of us with private health insurance are seeing ever increasing deductibles along with other up-front costs before insurance will even consider providing coverage. In addition, from 2017 to 2019 the number of uninsured in the United States grew from 26.2 million to 28.9 million. This can only be seen as a loss of 2.2 million customers for the insurance industry. The CDC mirrored these losses by reporting the ranks of the uninsured increased to 32.8 million by 2020. So, on one hand we have seen an explosion in the cost of healthcare, while on the other hand, we appear to have witnessed a declining healthcare insurance market. - - - So, one might reasonably conclude that the hospitals and other providers of the healthcare, along with the healthcare insurance companies, are struggling to survive. Just like you and me, all struggling to survive the out-of-control cost of healthcare. However, even the most casual observer can see that those providing the healthcare and insurance we need are awash in cash and profit.

In the March 4, 2013, edition of Time magazine, Steven Brill did a masterful job of describing what is going on inside the American Healthcare System. According to Brill, it has become *"a uniquely American gold rush — from Stanford, Conn., to Marlton, N.J., to Oklahoma City . . . ."* Brill goes on to report that *"the American health care market has transformed tax-exempt nonprofit hospitals into the town's most profitable business and largest employers, often presided over by the region's most richly compensated executives."* The New York Times, in a lead article, provided another excellent example of this transformation. The Times reported that in 2007 the Bayonne Medical Center was a bankrupt hospital in *"a faded blue-collar town 11 miles from Midtown Manhattan."* Today that same hospital charges the highest rates in the region and its profits have "soared."

But, we don't have to rely on the words of reporters. We can readily see what drove Steven Brill and New York Times to publish the articles cited above. While visiting Houston, Mr. Brill noticed a group of glass skyscrapers lighting up the evening sky. *"The scene looked like Dubai,"* reported Brill. It was, in fact, the Texas Medical Center with 280 buildings sitting on nearly 1,300 acres. It's one of Houston's largest employers. I had the same experience while attending a conference at the University of Pennsylvania Medical Center. Stretching out over untold blocks of downtown Philadelphia and boasting the most modern and expensive construction – the size and grandeur of the facility was amazing. And, just this weekend, my wife and I visited what should have been a small local hospital in Chester County, Pennsylvania and were amazed to see the size and splendor of the atrium that serves as the entrance to the facility. In total, the construction we are witnessing in healthcare facilities across the country literally screams money and power.

However, this is only the obvious part of what has become one of the most dominant parts of our nation's economy. Comprising roughly twenty percent of the nation's GDP, the healthcare industry will generate upwards of four trillion dollars of revenue in the coming year. And, to ensure this flood of money keeps pouring in, the healthcare industry is spending on the order of $5.4 billion lobbying Congress as compared to roughly $2 billion by the defense and aerospace industries, and $1.5 billion by oil and gas interests. Furthermore, given the creativity of the U.S. corporate world, along with the size and scope of the healthcare market, you and I can be absolutely certain the American Healthcare System has its sights set on keeping the money pouring in, i.e., pouring in out of your pocket and mine.

The size and scope of this flood of money and profit can't be argued unless one is completely blind. We can't drive through any community in the country without seeing countless new drugstores, doctor's offices, clinics and additions to existing hospitals. All new healthcare construction that you and I are expected to pay for. And, pay for royally! So please turn a deaf ear to what our politicians are promising in the way of lowering the cost of healthcare. That ship has sailed. What we are left with is a table set to only allow the cost of healthcare to grow while our access to adequate and affordable healthcare grows progressively worse.

Compounding the problem is the fact that the United States has tied itself lock stock and barrel to the success of a "PRIVATE" healthcare system. A private sector system that, like all private sector business, views higher prices as the primary means of delivering the financial performance demanded by the investment community. Pricing that has the U. S. spending four times what other advanced nations spend per person to administer their systems.

Interestingly, we just don't hear a lot of complaints about government health insurance, i.e., Medicare, Tricare and Medicaid. These forms of Government health insurance provide coverage for something like 40 percent of the country. So, if there is a problem with government insurance, we should be hearing about it. But, we're not. Instead, the complaints about health insurance are focused on the private system, where the right to care and coverage is being secretly placed at the discretion of the healthcare insurance industry and their "Big Lie."

"Misleading" from the Start

I've written about many things over my fifty-some years of formal writing, but I have never had a problem knowing how to label what I was writing about. However, I certainly have one here.

If I call what you and I are asked to view as health "INSURANCE," I support the belief that what we have is actually "insurance." And, in doing so, I contribute to the belief that our supposed health insurance is just like all the other forms of insurance in our life. Namely, it's just like our car insurance, fire insurance, and home owner's insurance. In other words, we owe whatever our insurance fails to pay.

However, as will be explained in detail throughout the book, what you and I are led to view as health "insurance," isn't even close to an insurance product. In fact, it's completely different from all the other forms of insurance we purchase. A far more accurate name for what we have is a healthcare "PLAN," i.e., a plan in which we are simply a member.

The healthcare insurance industry even agrees with me,

because it's the term they use in all their formal and legal documentation for what we are supposed to view as health "insurance." Simply put, they advertise health "Insurance," but they only deliver a healthcare "Plan." So, it's "insurance" when they sell it, but a "plan" when they fail to deliver the care and coverage that "insurance" would require.

Which leads me to having to credit the healthcare insurance industry for their cleverness. On one hand, they have succeeded in having themselves labeled as an "insurance" company. And, in so doing, qualified for all the tax and regulatory benefits due an insurance company. However, when it comes to serving you and me, they fall back to only providing a healthcare "PLAN." Thus escaping the contractual structure, benefits and liability that insurance would require.

The bottom line is that we can't refer to our supposed health "insurance" as insurance without contributing to the "Big Lie" in the American Healthcare System, i.e., we owe whatever our insurance fails to pay. However, I find myself not having much choice here as the term "insurance" has become so broadly accepted that anything else only adds to the confusion the book is trying to avoid.

So, the book will do its best to call out the "Big Lie" while having to regularly refer to the healthcare "PLAN" that you and I have, as "insurance."- - - Confusing I know. But, it should be clear by now that promoting confusion is at the heart of the American Healthcare System's billing system. Consequently, all this author can do is his very best to untie the "Gordian Knot" that the American Healthcare System has created to support their "Big Lie."

A "Growing" Creativity

Before I get accused of claiming everyone in the American Healthcare System is part of some grand conspiracy to fleece the American public, let me state very clearly that this is not my intent or the goal of the book. Most of the people working in healthcare have dedicated their life to serving the public. In fact, it's what drove most of them to pursue a career in healthcare and keeps them serving us day in and day out. The recent Covid Pandemic couldn't have provided stronger proof of this dedication to serving the public. And, nowhere is this dedication more evident than in our doctors and hospitals. These are, for the most part, great people driven by the highest principles of service. They are also people caught-up in a system far greater than they are – people simply doing their best to serve you and me given the constraints placed on them by the American Healthcare System and the insurance industry.

This dedication to service is exemplified by the nation's doctors. I can honestly say I have yet to meet a doctor who hasn't made the needs of his or her patient the primary goal in every decision he or she makes. However, our doctors are caught in a system over which they have little control. How often have we heard of a doctor expressing frustration over having his or her hands tied by an insurance company? How often have we heard our own doctor anguish over the time spent pursuing coverage that should never be in question? In fact, at the start of my last appointment with my doctor who had to see me after hours to fit me in, he began by describing how frustrated he was by the limited time he was allowed to spend with a patient. A decision that is being forced on him by the large corporate healthcare holding company that now owns the practice that employs him as simply one of their many employees. A practice that he had owned with two other doctors prior to selling it to the large healthcare holding company. And, a healthcare reality that is literally stripping the dedicated professionals in the healthcare system of their freedom to serve us under a banner of reducing costs.

However, nowhere is the cost of healthcare a more obvious concern than in the boardrooms of the nation's healthcare insurance companies. For, they are the ones that pay something like 70 percent of the cost of U. S. healthcare. And, the ones Congress assigned the task of reining-in these rising costs. So, what should we expect as a reasonable response by any profit motivated insurance company to these market realities? Costs that they have little control over and a stock market driven solely by profit. They ration the care we are allowed to receive, and reduce the coverage for what we do receive.

There isn't anything magic here, because it's all just simple math, i.e., business math and accounting 101. It's also easily seen in the everyday reports of the media and the anguish of the folks around us as they struggle to access affordable healthcare. In fact, Rohit Choopre, Director of the CFPB stated on July 11, 2023 that seven out of ten Americans say they have been *"asked to pay a bill that should have been covered by their health insurance."*

Yet, as strange as it may seem, I need to extend the dedication to serving the public that I assigned to the providers of healthcare, to the healthcare insurance industry. Yes, insurance companies are responsible for the misrepresentation and out-right fraud in our healthcare system and the reason for the book. However, that misrepresentation and structural fraud in the System have been driven more by the evolution of healthcare in the United States than by any grand conspiracy within the healthcare insurance industry. Evolution that carries with it two realities: 1.) The need to make money in our private sector free market healthcare system, and 2.) A mandate from Congress that the insurance industry use its power to slow the growth of healthcare costs in the country. Two realities that have driven insurers to pursue policies that only deliver the most cost effective healthcare rather that the most medically appropriate care as determined by "our" doctor. These are fundamentally conflicting goals that put our nation's doctors and the healthcare insurance industry at cross purposes – cross purposes driven by our nation's choice of private insurance rather than the government based single payer system found in other western nations. But, I digress.

The truth is that all nations have a fundamental need to ration healthcare. That's because no nation can afford to pay for all the healthcare their people would like to receive. And, where you have a single payer government system, the government can simply decide how much it's willing to spend and then limit the delivery of healthcare to that budgeted amount by spreading the money equally across its population.

Private health insurance is an entirely different matter. There can't be a budgeted limit on what the country spends in a particular year any more than we can limit what people spend to buy new cars in a given year. For example, where the single payer system can refuse to pay for expensive end-of-life care, opting instead to simply make a person comfortable, the private system has no such inherent ability to limit the cost of the care it provides. Our private system is driven by market forces that demand we pursue every possible treatment with a potential to extend life. In fact, that's the professional and legal obligation of every doctor in the country. Furthermore, our private system actually encourages doctors to market the benefits of, say knee replacement surgery, to a patient who isn't even considering having their knee replaced.

The bottom line is that there will always be a greater demand for healthcare service than any nation can afford to spend. This is particularly true for patients who are at the end of life and demanding that o-so-expensive hail-Mary procedure that just "might" buy them a bit more time.

So, now that we understand that all nations have to ration healthcare in order to manage the cost, how does the American Healthcare System do it? And, we can be 100 percent certain they are doing it because the U. S. Supreme Court has unanimously ruled that it's the very basis of our private healthcare insurance system. But, how? How can we ration healthcare in the United States when our market has no interest in rationing healthcare and the American Healthcare System has no inherent ability to ration it? - - - We hide it!

In fact, we hide it in plain sight. We make the issue one of appropriate coverage as determined by an insurance company, rather than a determination of appropriate care as determined by "OUR" doctor.

We make the "PUBLIC" issue entirely a determination of appropriate coverage where the U. S. Supreme Court has unanimously ruled that insurers have a fundamental right to deny coverage. - - - However, the insurance industry then demonstrates its superb creativity by "SECRETLY" implementing "coverage" as a denial of "ALL" payment. That's right. Our insurer contractually bars their in-network providers from accepting any form of payment for care that has been denied coverage. Thus cutting off "ALL" forms of payment when coverage is denied. And, that includes you and me as well. Because the provider is contractually barred from even allowing us to pay for the care.

Insurers create a public image of "coverage," while the real issue is a denial of "payment" for the care being denied and rationed. All the while denying that "ANY" rationing is taking place. Which is the polite way of saying that the American Healthcare System and our politicians are lying through their teeth to keep you and me misled and fighting the wrong war.

One leading healthcare insurer goes so far as to advertise that, *"We understand how important it is to earn the trust of all with whom we have contact."* It's a misrepresentation that grows progressively worse as the healthcare insurance industry makes evermore "creative" departures from the truth and the law to ration the care we need and are owed under the guise of appropriately denying coverage.

I heard a line on the Michael Smerconish radio show a while back that so effectively characterizes the insurance industry's pursuit of lower costs and higher profits that I just have to steal it. **"The problem isn't so much what they have done, but that they have gotten so very good at doing it."** Stating it in layman's terms, the problem isn't what the healthcare insurance industry has done to ration healthcare, it's that they've gotten so creative in denying the care and coverage we are "ACTUALLY" owed.

However, being highly creative isn't the only reason for the insurance industry's growing ability to deny the care and coverage we are owed. The more important arrow in the industry's quiver is power, pure political power as well as financial power.

When the Chief of Staff for the Chair of The House Sub Committee on Health of the U. S. Congress calls you on the phone to say *"Who the fxxk do you think you are"* - - - *"you can forget any thoughts of testifying before Congress,"* which is exactly what the gentleman said to me in his opening remarks, <u>after his boss had admitted the existence of the hidden contractual language cited in the book</u>, you can be damn sure you've hit a raw nerve, a nerve where those in power make it extremely clear they would rather see you and me fleeced than have to confront the misrepresentation and fraud in the American Healthcare System. - - - I trust it won't come as any great surprise that I never got to testify to Congress.

No Simple Fix "BUT"

I had a rather long and successful career interpreting Operating Permits for large chemical operations across the country. My success was largely based on an insistence that these permits covered nothing more, and nothing less, than the specific wording contained in a permit. In short, a requirement was either clearly spelled out or it wasn't – very similar to a four-corners reading of a private contract. The contract either states a provision explicitly or it doesn't. And, if it doesn't, then the point doesn't apply regardless of how long and well-argued the merits of a particular point may be. Conversely, if a provision is clearly spelled-out, then it's enforceable regardless of any inconvenience or pain it may cause one or more of the parties to the agreement.

It's this same principle of enforceability that drove me to write my first book on healthcare and has driven me ever since. This includes writing what will be my fourth and last book on the American Healthcare System in an effort to disclose the "explicit" language contained in the American Healthcare System's Provider Agreements that defines the care and coverage we are actually "OWED" from our health insurance. However, this last book contains something that my earlier books could not. Because the recent actions of the CFPB allow the book to provide a simple risk free means of short circuiting the System's fraudulent healthcare bills. In essence, we can now turn the System back on itself by allowing no simple fix other than to void our bill.

For you and me, the question of what we should be assured of receiving from are our health insurance is actually a pretty simple one. We just need to get the care our doctor prescribes as necessary healthcare and have the cost of the care covered. Period, end of discussion. In fact, that's how we have been led to view the entire purpose of our private health insurance system.

However, our leaders in Washington have long failed to see the issues surrounding healthcare as anything approaching that simple. For, while we as individuals have been focused on getting the care and coverage we need and believe we are owed, Washington has been focused on reining-in what Congress sees as the unacceptable rising cost of healthcare. And, just as it is for any businesses or program, there is no better way of cut costs than to deliver less of whatever it is you're selling. In the case of healthcare, that can only mean restricting the care and coverage we are allowed to receive, i.e., rationing.

While the task of reining-in the cost of healthcare that may seem simple on its face, I can assure you it created a huge bump in the road for the healthcare insurance industry. That's because the laws of the country make it abundantly clear that: 1.) Only "OUR" doctor can determine the healthcare we need, 2.) Doctors can be held libel for delivering anything less than the care we need, and 3.) "Insurance" requires that there be a contract between us and the insurer guaranteeing the coverage we are owed. Three well settled points of law.

So, I ask you. How can our healthcare insurance company be so free to deliver less care than our doctor believes we need, escape any liability for delivering that reduced level of care and completely ignore the need for a signed contract guaranteeing the coverage you and I are owed under any accepted legal definition for insurance?

The answer is a complex and deliberate mix of misrepresentation and fraud that has been carefully laid at the core of the American Healthcare System and what we have been led to believe is our very own health "insurance" – a complex mixture of misrepresentation and fraud that negates any form of a simple fix. It's also a cold hard reality that keeps those with any power to fix the System on the sidelines fearing that disclosure could bring down the roof on the System, and more than likely prove to be career ending. Our leaders opting for deception and self-preservation rather than a sense of honesty and any form of reasonable justice.

However, do not dismay! For, while the fix for the American Healthcare System may be out of reach for the nation, the fix for you and me isn't. That's because the magnitude of the misrepresentation and fraud in the System is so great that it opens the door to a serious threat of total collapse if anyone in the System is forced to disclose the explicitly worded terms and conditions in the insurance industry's Provider Agreements – terms and conditions that "explicitly" contradict the System's "Big Lie" and guarantee that we receive the care "OUR" doctor believes we need.

It's essentially the same situation that I faced when I was interpreting industrial Operating Permits. All I had to do there was insist on a careful reading of a permit, and that any requirements contained in a permit be "exactly" as stated. Nothing more and nothing less.

The same can to be said for the insurance industry's Provider Agreements. Because, any careful reading of these Agreements will strip an insurer of the right to: 1.) Deliver anything less than the care "our" doctor prescribes as necessary healthcare and 2.) Bar billing us for whatever our insurer fails to pay for that necessary care.

I offer the following example to hopefully drive home the point I am trying to make. My son had agreed to help a friend renovate the 3rd floor of his home. Well, late one afternoon I get this frantic phone call for help. They have removed a wall on the 3rd floor and the roof is collapsing. "Dad, what should we do?" My answer was quick and simple. Put the wall back. The owner of the house simply couldn't afford even the risk of having the roof come down. So, while the owner of the home might have been married to his plan to remodel the house, he would have to modify that plan to avoid the "risk" of having the roof collapse.

Simply put, the American Healthcare System can't afford even the possibility of having the roof come down. The cost of such a collapse would be far too great to absorb. Furthermore, there isn't a chance in the world that the laws establishing our doctor as the one solely responsible for determining the healthcare we need are going to change. That's a given. So, the System is going to have to live with that reality. Or, as the title of this section puts it, there can be no "simple fix" for the System because the "Big Lie" only survives through deliberate misrepresentation and fraud. And, just like the wall in the home of my son's friend, anything that threatens the integrity of the roof <u>needs to be avoided</u>.

Simply put, the insurance industry has to find a way to deliver less and less care and coverage to meet the demands of

Congress. That can only mean that they will have to continue: 1.) Ignoring the explicitly worded provisions of their Provider Agreements, 2.) Insisting on the right to overrule our doctor and 3.) Allowing their in-network providers to improperly bill us for whatever our insurer fails to pay for the care we receive. All things we are going to have to live with. All things for which there can be no "simple fix." But, all things for which the no simple fix means that they are things that the American Healthcare System, and in particular the healthcare insurance industry, can't afford to have openly questioned. Because there is "No Simple Fix."

HOWEVER! And it's a very big however. We need to remember that while we may be only a single individual standing up against a 4-trillion dollar healthcare system when we dispute a healthcare bill, we can carry a mighty bat if we step to the plate and use the FDCPA and the CFPB to demand disclosure of the rationing and billing practices that are so "explicitly" at odds with the insurance industry's hidden Provider Agreements. That said, the reader shouldn't think for one moment that the American Healthcare System will fully surrender to such a threat. For, there is no amount of money that the players won't spend to maintain the status quo and keep the money pouring in.

Therefore, because there is no "Simple Fix" to the American Healthcare System, the FDCPA, along with the advice of the CFPB, need to be viewed as a double edge sword. On one hand, the two can provide the leverage we need to force a decision on whether a particular bill is worth enforcing – a simple and isolated question of whether it's simply cheaper to eat a particular bill. However, overplaying that consideration by addressing the system as a whole will undoubtedly attract the resources of a four trillion dollar market focused entirely on preserving the System. A four trillion dollar market that will dwarf the cost of any particular bill that a provider may choose to foist on us. And, fortunate for us, a four trillion dollar market that has no "Simple Fix." Consequently, we can rather easily put the System in the position where the right business decision is to simply walk away from our one particular bill, because there is no "Simple Fix."

Chapter II

*"Many a small thing has been made
large by the right kind of advertising:"*
Mark Twain

The Plan They Promote

We can't go anywhere without being exposed to an advertisement for health insurance. Magazines, TV, our car radio, and the well-placed billboards we pass on the way to work — all dedicated to showing us the miracles of modern-day healthcare that are so readily available from a healthcare insurance company.

Enhanced by the finest graphics, text, and sound, these advertisements assure us of plans designed to meet our every need. Plans that give every appearance of guaranteeing ready access to the most affordable, reliable, and highest-quality healthcare modern day technology can provide. You *"can make better healthcare decisions with our guidance"* (Cigna Health Group); We are *"always here when you need us"* (Kaiser Permanente); *"Humana helps you put your needs first"* (Humana Health Insurance); *"The most admired health insurance"* (Aetna); *"The best combination of health care and value"* (Wellpoint Inc.); *"Live fearlessly"* (Independence Blue Cross); and on and on.

The bottom line is that healthcare insurance companies go to great lengths to describe their plans as providing: 1.) Our very own health "insurance" 2.) Our own doctor, 3.) Ready access to all the healthcare we will ever need, 4.) The highest quality care, and 5.) A plan designed to meet our specific needs. So, what more could we want when it comes to assuring access to the healthcare we are all likely to need at some point in life?

This is the public face of the American Healthcare System. The face that the healthcare insurance companies want us to see and believe. The one that heralds the superiority of American healthcare, while remaining completely silent on the rationing that lies at the core of the American Healthcare System and its "Big Lie." Rationing that is responsible for ensuring we only see a doctor half as often as other western nations, while spending twice as much on healthcare. And, a "Big Lie" designed to pass the cost of seeing a doctor on to us whenever our insurer decides to deny some or all of the cost of seeing a doctor.

However, in closed-door meetings outside the view of you, me and the public, these same healthcare insurance companies promote their plans very differently. That's because the vast majority of health insurance and plans are sold to employers rather than individuals. Employers that are far more interested in the "cost" of the insurance they purchase for their employees. Cost typically measured in terms of the "efficiency" of a particular plan in controlling an employee's access to healthcare <u>in order to reduce the overall cost of a plan</u>.

Quoting from a report published by the National Conference on Efficiency in Health Care, the *"skyrocketing cost of health care is not sustainable if employers are to continue insuring employees"* and *"there is a perception that the lack of efficiency is driving unnecessary costs in health care"* and *"There is increasing pressure for employers to measure efficiency."*

A finding of the Kaiser Family Foundation mirrors this same concern about "efficiency." It reported that *"premiums for family coverage cost an average of $7,061 in 2001 and rose to an average of $22,221 in 2021."* An increase of 215 percent compared to a 57 percent rate of inflation, leading Forbes to conclude that *"premiums will continue to increase"* and choosing plans with *"increasing deductibles is a key means of managing these increasing premiums."*

The simple truth is that insurers sell their plans to two very different groups. The first and far larger group is comprised of the nation's employers who purchase the vast majority of health insurance in the country. The second group is comprised of individuals who are unable to access an employer's plan and have to buy a plan on their own. These are two very different groups with very different needs. However, they both want the public image of the insurance they purchase to be one of promising all the quality healthcare an individual will ever need.

In essence, both groups want a vision of "your" plan, "your" doctor, and "your" affordable access to the finest healthcare technology can provide. Consequently, that's exactly what we get. That's the image the healthcare insurance industry promotes to the public at a cost of over 200 million dollars a year, which leaves insurers completely free to promote the "efficiency" of their plans in their closed-door meetings with employers.

One image behind closed-doors where insurers promote the "efficiency" of their plans to ration the care and coverage we "can" receive. And, a very different and highly promoted public image that gives the appearances of guaranteeing all the highest quality healthcare we will ever need. - - - These are two very different images. But, there is only one that the American Healthcare System wants us to see and believe.

Chapter III

The Plan They "Hide"

The easiest way to explain why healthcare insurance companies have to hide the truth about the care and coverage we
are owed from our health insurance is to provide a comparison
with automobile insurance. At first glance, one could reasonably assume that both serve the same purpose, i.e., to protect
us from an unexpected cost. In the case of health insurance, the
unexpected costs are for the healthcare we need to return to
full health. In the case of automobile insurance, the unexpected
costs are for the work needed to return our automobile to its
undamaged condition. So, both would seem to be designed to
protect us from the unexpected cost of getting back to where we
were. However, this is where that little problem of cost gets far
more difficult for health insurance.

While both forms of insurance have to limit coverage to
what is needed for a particular claim, only the automobile insurer is free to determine exactly what that is. The automobile
insurer can simply send its adjuster into a body shop, inspect
the damaged vehicle and decide exactly what it will take to re-
pair the damage. By contrast, the healthcare insurer has no such
freedom or ability. The laws of every state reserve the determination of "necessary and appropriate" health care to a properly

licensed "attending" physician (our doctor). Furthermore, the automobile insurer is only required to return our damaged vehicle to its pre-accident condition, and the cost cannot exceed the fair market value of a similar undamaged vehicle. In short, the automobile insurance company has hard and fast costs as well as a cap on the total cost with which to manage a claim.

A healthcare insurance company faces a far more challenging reality. Here, the goal must always be to return us to "full" health, regardless of our age or condition. And, only "our" doctor can decide what that is and what's required to get us there. Furthermore, under the laws of every state in the country, once treatment is begun, it has to be continued until it's either complete or no longer of value as determined by "our" doctor.

However, the most important difference between these two forms of insurance is the healthcare insurer's inability to establish exactly what needs to be done to properly treat us. That's because appropriate healthcare has proven to be *"notoriously difficult, if not impossible, to define"* (The Futility of Medical Necessity, E. Haavi Morreim, University of Tennessee) and *"when it comes to selecting the appropriate level of care, medical necessity trumps everything else"* (A Refresher on Medical Necessity, Peter R. Jensen, MD, CPC).

Consequently, the laws of every state assign the authority for determining "necessary and appropriate" healthcare to the attending physician (our doctor) – not some remote employee, insurance company doctor, or outside consultant.

Unfortunately, while the law may be on our side for determining the healthcare we need, we have all heard far too many reports of patients being denied coverage for the care prescribed by their doctor as absolutely necessary – far too many reports of insurers overruling a doctor to limit the care and coverage the insurer has to provide – far too many stories of insurers' denying coverage as simply too expensive. And, may I say it? Far too many stories of insurers rationing lifesaving care over the strenuous objections of a patient's doctor.

So, how is it that healthcare insurance companies can so easily circumvent the law? How can they substitute their "business" judgment on the appropriate cost of our healthcare for the "medical" judgment of our doctor? How can they ignore our right to receive the care our doctor says we need?

The answer is that we are "NEVER" allowed to see the details of our plan. *"My gut tells me that the PR nightmare wouldn't be worth the problems an explicit cost-effectiveness criterion might entail"* for limiting coverage (Judy Wagner of the Congressional Office of Technology Assessment). Or, as Charley Brown would say, "They hide the football."

"Do not be fooled when the health insurance industry claims that it has abandoned its old practices" of denying care, and *"private health insurance is a labyrinth of misleading terms of art designed to help companies minimize coverage and maximize profits"* (Congressional testimony of whistleblowers Dr. Linda Peeno and Wendell Potter, respectively). Both are accomplished professionals who served at the highest levels of management in the healthcare insurance industry and witnessed firsthand the practices and policies that the healthcare insurance industry uses to ration the healthcare and coverage you and I are allowed to receive. All while hiding the true nature of our so-called health insurance.

It's "Not" Your Plan

"Individuals with health insurance do not own or control" their plans *"in the same way that they own and control auto insurance, homeowners' or life insurance. For most Americans their employers own the policy"* (Edwin J. Feulner, the former President of The Heritage Foundation). *"Until you pointed it out, I would have thought I owned my plan"* (retired Judge Harry J. Farmer).

To own something, we need to have a bill of sale, a contract, policy, or some form of proof that demonstrates ownership. You and I have nothing close to this when it comes to our so-called health insurance. Where automobile insurance, homeowners' insurance, and life insurance all provide us with a signed and enforceable contract or policy, our so-called health insurance does no such thing. The inescapable conclusion is that the plan we are asked to view as our very own health insurance is not in any way ours. Period! And, if it's not ours, then the "right" to receive the care and coverage that we are led to expect really isn't ours either.

However, to illustrate just how far insurers are willing to go to encourage us to view our healthcare plan as our very own, consider the following. Since you and I don't have any ownership in a healthcare plan, we really lack the necessary standing to sue our insurance company for breach of contract in failing to deliver the care and coverage we have been led to expect. After all, if there is no signed contract or policy with our name on it, there can't be any ownership or breach of contract. Even so, insurers have shown themselves surprisingly willing to be the defendant in a breach of contract suit rather than pursue summary judgment based on the lack any ownership in a plan, and therefore the absence of any standing to sue.

In my case, this willingness to accept the role of defendant lasted the better part of eight years. So, while I can only guess why Sandy's insurer was willing to subject themselves to years of costly litigation, I have to believe it was for two reasons: 1.) Insurers want us to view their plans as our very own so that we don't sue our employer who is a highly valued customer of the insurer, and 2.) Insurers don't want to have these suits redirected to an employer that would lack both the knowledge and willingness to defend the misrepresentation and fraud in the System.

For proof of just who owns these health plans we need only look to the law. In order to protect the rights of employees, Congress passed the Retiree Employment Income Security Act (ERISA) in 1979. The Act not only makes employers the owner of these healthcare plans, but makes the management of the plans a fiduciary duty of the employer.

The bottom line is that we do "NOT" own the healthcare plan that we look to for the care and coverage we will need in life. Whether we get our plan as an employee benefit or purchase it directly from a healthcare insurance company, we are simply paying for a "MEMBERSHIP" in someone else's plan. It's very similar to joining the YMCA. As long as someone pays the monthly fee for our membership, we get to use the facilities. Nothing more, and absolutely "no" right of ownership.

It's Not "Insurance"

As shown earlier, our so-called health insurance doesn't meet the legal definition of insurance. In fact, there is nothing in the book that is more important to understand than this fundamental truth about the American Healthcare System. Because, if our so-called health "insurance" doesn't meet the legal definition for insurance, then the entire argument that we owe whatever our insurance fails to pay is a myth designed solely to allow the healthcare insurance industry to pay as little as they want, whenever they want, and pass whatever hasn't been paid onto you and me.

The incontrovertible truth is that our supposed health "insurance" is both actually and legally a Third Party Purchaser of the healthcare services that we receive – just as long as we get our healthcare in-network. In fact, the professionals charged with overseeing our so-called health insurance, along with the healthcare providers in the American Healthcare System, are very careful to describe it exactly that way.

*"It is understood that you assume the financial responsibility of paying for all services rendered either through **third-party** payers (your insurance company), or being personally responsible for payment for any services which are not covered by your insurance."* This is a direct quote from a notice prominently posted at the entrance to the emergency room of a major hospital just outside Philadelphia, Pennsylvania. And, on the East Coast, you just don't get any bigger than this particular healthcare provider.

Please note the hierarchy of the terms the provider has chosen for its explanation of financial responsibility. Because, it's a hierarchy that can only have been chosen by this provider and then carefully reviewed by the provider's very capable legal department. In fact, there is probably no better example of the deliberate misrepresentation of financial responsibility and the "Big Lie" than this simple notice of financial responsibility that is so prominently posted at the entrance to the hospital's emergency room.

Now, I really hope you can see this posting as informative as I do. Because, to ensure that the notice is legally correct, the hospital and its attorneys have chosen to use *"third-party payers"* to define what we are to view as health "insurance." Then, to ensure that our take-away from the notice is that we owe whatever our "insurance" doesn't pay, the hospital adds *"(your insurance company)"* to clarify their legally correct "third-party payer" definition. In short, the provider wants to have it both ways. It wants to be legally correct with its *"third-party payer,"* definition. But, ensure that we view what we have as "insurance" to reinforce the message that we owe whatever hasn't been paid for the care we receive.

Just some subtle differences in language you say? Payer versus insurance. I'm sorry, but no way! However, rather than having to take my word for it, let's take a closer look at the provider's choice of words to explain what we would owe on a healthcare bill.

The use of the term "Third-party Payer" assumes our so-called health insurance is doing <u>nothing</u> more than paying for the care we receive. But, we know that isn't true. Our so-called health "insurance" company contracts directly with their in-network providers to deliver the care we need. In fact, it's the entire purpose of the state mandated Provider Agreements – agreements designed to make an in-network provider a contracted arm of our so-called insurance company. In fact, it's the entire point of being an "in-network" provider.

Furthermore, less than 7 percent of all healthcare billing is out of network. Which means that 93 percent of all the healthcare delivered in the United States is delivered under the terms of a Provider Agreement, i.e., terms that are designed to allow an insurer to control the care, quality and cost of what we get. And, anyone who doubts this level of control over the healthcare we get really needs to read the Provider Agreement at the back of the book. It's an agreement that grants an insurer essentially unlimited control over the care we receive, the quality of the care and all the billing related to what we receive. Furthermore, the negotiated prices that we are entitled to receive are in an attachment at the back of these Provider Agreements. Therefore, like the Agreements, these prices are something we will never be allowed to see.

Consequently, it's much more accurate to describe our

so-called health insurance as a Third Party **Purchaser** of the healthcare we receive. Very similar to our large Philadelphia hospital's *"third-party payer"* definition. But, wait a minute. Our supposed health "insurance" is doing a lot more than simply paying for the care we get.

And, here is where the fraud in the American Healthcare System really raises its ugly head. Because a PAYER is not the same as a PURCHASER.

If our plan, and so-called health insurance, is only a **"PAYER,"** they bear no responsibility for the healthcare we receive. They are simply paying the bill for whatever care we get. However, if they are the **"PURCHASER"** of the care we get, as their Provider Agreements clearly dictate that they are, then they bear direct responsibility for both the care we get and the liability that comes with it.

Returning to our example of a builder – by subcontracting (PURCHASING) the work needed to build a house, the builder takes on direct responsibility and liability for the work performed. However, if we look to a bank or mortgage company that is simply PAYING for the work, there is no responsibility or liability for the quality or appropriateness of the work performed.

The bottom line is that our so-called health insurance wants to be seen as both "insurance" and simply a PAYER to eliminate all liability for the quality and appropriateness of the healthcare we receive. However, they secretly hold their in-network providers to the terms of a Provider Agreement (as a PURCHESER) that gives the insurer absolute control over what we get and how it's billed.

The comparison is just as damning if we compare our supposed health insurance with any of the other forms of insurance in our life. Take fire insurance in the event our house burns down. Our fire insurance doesn't contract the work needed to rebuild the house. The fire insurer simply gives us a check to cover the damage. And, so it is with every form of insurance, except our so-called health insurance.

No. - - - What you and I have isn't "insurance." Rather, the term is being forced on us to provide cover for the fraud and con in the American Healthcare System that's designed to ensure we habitually fight the wrong war when denied the care and coverage we are owed. To have us believe the "Big Lie" so deeply that we never even think to question the premise that we owe whatever our healthcare insurer or plan fails pay. In fact, it has to be history's most successful example of the old con of watch my left hand while my right hand steals you blind.

Now, I'm not an attorney, but I do have some legal experience. In fact, a senior attorney at a fortune 500 company once commented that I've had more actual court experience than he has had over his long career. - - - I sight this only to make a point, and not to claim any great knowledge of the law or the court system. That point is that my experience has taught me one very hard-won lesson. An issue, no matter how morally just, is baseless in court unless it has legal standing. Consequently, pushing back to get the coverage we are owed, as though we are dealing with an actual insurance company, will rob us of any legal standing in the matter and effectively guarantee a losing fight. And, most importantly, the American Healthcare System is doing its very best to guarantee we make that critical mistake.

Not Even **Your** "Doctor"

If you sued your health-care insurance company for breach of contract and then discovered that your attorney had a secret contract with the insurer, it would be a very big deal. You would have every right to demand a mistrial, sue the attorney for malpractice, and insist the bar association strip the attorney of his or her license to practice law. It's a conflict of interest in the attorney-client relationship that the judicial system simply will not tolerate.

Unfortunately, you and I face this same conflict of interest when we consult with an in-network doctor that we are told to view as "OUR" doctor. A doctor the American Medical Association, the American Healthcare System and the law insist is our very own because of the required relationship of reliance, faith, confidence, and fiduciary duty that a doctor is to provide. These are the very same elements that comprise the attorney-client relationship.

But, how can that be true? How can an in-network doctor be

"OUR" doctor when they have a secret contract (Provider Agreement) that allows an insurer to have full control over the care, quality and cost of what we receive in the way of healthcare? A fact that can't be argued because every in-network doctor has to sign a Provider Agreement to be an in-network provider. In fact, it's the law in every state in the country. And, for those of you who would question my use of the word *"secret"* in referring to these Provider Agreements, please ask your doctor, plan, so-called insurance company, or even your state department of insurance for a copy of the Provider Agreement that pertains to your plan. Then stand back and watch the dance as they try to explain why they won't share it with you. And, so long as you have a sense of humor, the explanation you get may even be entertaining. However, what I can assure you is that you won't be getting a copy of your doctor's Provider Agreement. That's because anyone with access to these Agreements is barred from even discussing them, let alone disclosing the specifics of the Agreements. Even though the Agreements are listed as a "public" document by your state and should be readily available to you and me as public information.

So, I ask you, if a document is filed with your state as a public document, but you and I aren't allowed to see it, what should we call it if not "secret?" And, how should we view what is supposedly "OUR" doctor when we know he or she has one of these secret Agreements with our insurance company. A contract that controls every aspect of our doctor's ability to fulfil the duty we are told to expect from our doctor. Read the Provider Agreement at the back of the book and judge for yourself.

The bottom line is that you are never going to see the Provider Agreement that your in-network doctor has signed with your insurance company. Not unless you are willing to commit to a lengthy court battle. It took me more than two years to win that fight. And even then, I was barred from disclosing what I was shown.

In fact, the only reason I have been able to provide a representative Provider Agreement at the back of the book is that I have read a number of these Agreements and can easily circumvent the ban on disclosure by "not" copying any particular

Agreement. That's because the Agreements are so similar that I can draft a representative Agreement that can't be tied to any one Agreement or insurer's intellectual property, but one that reflects the terms and conditions of all the nation's Provider Agreements.

However, there is an easier way to determine the control an insurance company has over our in-network doctor than by gaining access to his or her Provider Agreement. It's called the "Same Desk Principle." And, while this "Same Desk Principle" is specifically aimed at allowing the IRS to determine whether an employee has been properly retired, the determination hinges on establishing who is actually controlling the work product of an individual claiming to be retired or separated from their employer. The logic being that if an employer is controlling the work product of an individual, then the individual is an employee of that company, regardless of any claims of retirement or separation from the company.

In essence, the test looks at where an individual gets his or her direction for the work they are doing. So, if we apply the test to our in-network doctor, the answer becomes obvious. How often have we heard the stories of a doctor wanting to provide a particular type of healthcare and the insurance company denying it? The media is full of such stories. And, how about the need to get pre-approval for the care our doctor believes we need? Can there be any logic behind requiring pre-approval unless our insurer believes it has the right to overrule our doctor? And, of course there is the insurer's right to at any time conduct an in-depth quality review to ensure the doctor is complying with the insurer's standards for quality.

So, the answer to whether our doctor can be viewed as truly "OUR" doctor is far too obvious and one we instinctively know. Our in-network doctor is effectively a contract employee of our insurance company. And, as such, how can our doctor be "free" to deliver the healthcare we are owed within the duty of the doctor/patient relationship, if he or she can only get paid by following the wishes of our so-called insurance company? And, I assure you that is exactly where we are, thanks to the insurance industry's secret Provider Agreements.

However, as bad as this is, the relationship with our doctor is about to get worse. The American Healthcare System has decided they need to spread their in-network doctors over a larger number of patients to reduce the cost of healthcare. And, the best way to accomplish it is to triage doctors while increasing the use of the computer for determining the healthcare we need. Namely, we are to be given the advantage of having a team of doctors deliver our healthcare. No longer are we to have that one doctor who knows us personally and in my case considers me a friend. Instead, we are to get the doctor who is available at the time we need one and who will know us no better than the information in our computer healthcare file. Never mind that we already see a doctor only half as often as other western nations, and a doctor's visit is programed to last no more 15 minutes and address only one healthcare problem per appointment. Furthermore it's an appointment that will all-to likely take 3 weeks to schedule and have us seeing the doctor's assistant rather than the doctor.

But, if you can believe it, the American Healthcare System is proving it can be even more creative in separating us from the duty we expect from our doctor. They have yet another big surprise for us. They have completely, and very quietly, redefined the role of what we have long considered our family doctor.

When I was a younger me, certainly in the 1980s, my family doctor was my friend and the one I looked to for all the healthcare I might need. No, he wouldn't provide the most complicated surgery or the most technically demanding treatment, but he would be there to ensure that I got what I needed in the office, the office of a specialist or the hospital. In fact, he would be the one to admit me to the hospital and then oversee the care that I got while in the hospital.

Today, none of that is true. Our family doctor is now a "Primary Care Physician," or PCP, whose role has been reduced to only helping us "stay" healthy, and rendering only the most "basic" care. As I said to my good friend and doctor of more than 30 years, *You are a great doctor, but the System has cut your legs off.* To which he nodded yes and then just shook his head in frustration. He went on to explain that he can remember a time when he would have been fully involved in any care or hospitalization I needed. Now, he doesn't even have admission privileges to a hospital. Which forces his patients to admit themselves through the emergency room. But, the surprise gets even bigger! Since we now have to enter the hospital through the emergency room, the hospital can triage our problem as simply the most apparent problem when we entered the emergency room – treat only that problem – before discharging us back to our home with a recommendation to see our doctor. A doctor, Oh I'm so sorry! Please forgive my lapse of proper terminology – a Primary Care Physician, who most likely won't even know we were in the hospital and certainly won't be familiar with the care we received and might still need. - - - I mean, how can anything go wrong with a system like this?

I'm guessing you think my "how can anything go wrong" comment is a bit over the top. A bit too jaded and critical. But, I assure you it's not. Because, for something to go wrong in any system, there has to be a way to detect and document the failure or problem. In system design it's called a feedback loop. However, there is no such thing in this new system of in-and-out healthcare. Or as those in the System refer to it, **"Treat-em and Street-em."**

After all, the hospital did its job by addressing the problem identified in the emergency room. The hospital then washed its hands of whatever else might be wrong by discharging us back to a doctor who has been completely walled off from the care we received and might still need. So, the system is assured of being faultless – even if the patient dies because the hospital chose to **"Treat-em and Street-em."**

The bottom line is that we have lost our doctor to a System that we are being forced to accept purely on blind faith. Blind faith that has us being treated much like the age-old frog in a slowly heating pot of water. Never to understand the risk from the slowly heating water until it's too late to jump out of the pot. Because, like the frog, we are losing "OUR" doctor in the name of healthcare efficiency and progress, but to never be allowed to recognize the loss until it's too late to act. In fact, for most of us, we have already lost the only individual that had direct knowledge of our healthcare needs and a "duty" to see that they were met. My wife quite recently almost lost her life because of just this loss of her doctor and the **"Treat-em and Street-em"** approach to hospital care.

In the middle of a Sunday night, Angie woke me with what we thought was congestive heart failure. I rushed her to the hospital emergency room where she was quickly admitted. However, her PCP and cardiologist were not to play any role in the care and treatment she received. Instead, her care and treatment were determined solely by the doctors on-duty in the hospital. Doctors who would stabilize her heart, get her up and moving and then discharge her back to our home with the advice to see her doctor for any further care she might need – an appointment to see her doctor that took 3 weeks to schedule.

Unfortunately, my wife's problem wasn't her heart. She was bleeding to death internally. Bleeding that went completely untreated in the hospital. Bleeding that saw me having to rush her back to the hospital in critical condition. In fact, the only reason my wife and I believe she survived was that I demanded the right to participate directly in determining the care she needed. Participation that allowed me to insist the hospital address the actual problem, rather than simply assume it was her heart. Moreover, it was care and treatment that never saw her PCP or cardiologist consulted or informed of the care she received while in the hospital.

Two Definitions for "Coverage"

Covered Services, by law, precedent, and contract, are defined as the services that are *"available"* from a plan, "not" what a plan is willing to approve in any particular instance. It's somewhat like being assured you have a right to own a Ferrari sports car, while the likelihood of ever getting one goes completely undiscussed. Yes, a Ferrari is clearly "available" as something we are free to purchase. However, the likelihood of our ever purchasing one is an entirely different matter.

While this might seem to be a very trivial point to make, I assure you it is not. Particularly, when it comes to being assured of getting the care and coverage we are owed from our health insurance. In fact, it's a misunderstanding that the healthcare insurance industry exploits to keep you and me confused and fighting the wrong war. More specifically, it's a misunderstanding that robs us of our rights and distorts the entire appeal process for pursuing the care and coverage we are owed.

So, let's take a closer look at the term, Covered Services. Let's look at why our plan, insurance company, state insurance department and even our doctor are so anxious to have us pursue issues of "coverage" rather than our right to receive the care we need. Let's look at how a term that is so well understood by our plan, insurance company, state insurance department and even our doctor can be so misunderstood by you and me.

It all comes down to ensuring that we fight the wrong war. Because, as long as we do, our insurer and the American Healthcare System are guaranteed the ability to overrule our doctor and limit the care and coverage we receive, i.e. ration our healthcare. But, that's just the obvious side of the misrepresentation of covered services. For a better understanding we need to go back in history.

Regardless of all the political spin, no one can reasonably dispute the fact that the healthcare insurance industry rations health care. The *"inducement to ration care is the very point of any"* health insurance *"scheme"* and no insurance *"organization could survive without some incentive connecting physician reward with treatment rationing"* and *"the profit incentive to ration care"* goes *"to the very point of any health insurance"* (all quotes from Justice David H. Souter, U. S. Supreme Court in Pegram et al. v. Herdrich). However, it is equally true that the insurance industry views the use of the term *"rationing"* as something to be avoided at all costs. Insurers *"make decisions weighing costs against benefits. Justice Souter called that rationing, but there are other ways to talk about it"* (Karen Ignagni, president of the American Association of Health Plans). - - And, Justice Souter *"did not understand the use of the word ration. It's an unfortunate word, which implies that needed care is being cut back. I'd call it changing the incentives"* for *"appropriate"* care (Alan D. Bloom, senior vice president Maxicare Health Plans). *"The very word rationing is radioactive because it suggests that some patients are denied treatments they need"* (M. Gregg Bloche, Georgetown University Law Center). And, we need to be more *"up front in talking to patients about rationing"* (Dr. Steven D. Pearson, Harvard Medical School).

All this is a bit like the subject of premarital sex when I was growing up. So long as it wasn't discussed, we could all pretend it wasn't happening. However, premarital sex didn't have a four trillion-dollar industry committed to keeping the subject hidden and undiscussed. And, the U. S. Supreme Court didn't magically invent rationing for its Pegram v. Herdrich decision.

The truth is that rationing is a fundamental part of the American Healthcare System and the healthcare plan that you and I have. Whether it's an HMO, PPO, POS, HDHP or whatever, the care and coverage we are allowed to receive is a product of the "rationing" incorporated in the System's carefully hidden Provider Agreements.

So the question can't be one of whether there is rationing in the American Healthcare System, as so many of our politicians want to argue. But, rather the question of how is it carried out? And, how can something so obvious to those working in the System and the Supreme Court be so misunderstood by you and me along with the American public?

Like all complex issues, there is more than one answer. However, one of the most important factors is the System's "TWO" definitions for "Covered Services."

By advertising all the care we need, the healthcare insurance industry keeps us focused on our ability to receive that level of care. Then, by requiring pre-approval for what we can actually get, the insurer redirects the issue to a determination of what is the "appropriate" care for us to receive. Which then takes the form of merely a technical dispute between their doctor and ours and hijacks the entire question of the care we are owed.

It's really no different from the old con of bait and switch. By maintaining two definitions for "Covered Services" the insurer remains free to promise all the "Covered Services" we will ever need (Definition #1), while remaining free to limit "Covered Services" solely to what the insurer decides we need (Definition

#2). Definition #2 ostensibly becoming nothing more than the resolution of a technical dispute between their doctor and ours. **Coverage Exclusions:** *"expenses that are not payable under your plan in accordance with* (big insurer's name) *then current standard claim practices"* — this is a quote taken directly from the VERY small print in a published plan from a VERY big insurer that we are not supposed to see. It's also a clear demonstration of how a big name insurer is secretly demanding the right to both choose the care we will be "allowed" to receive, and the freedom to change their policy on what we can receive **whenever** they choose.

So, while the healthcare insurance industry heralds the cutting-edge healthcare that is available from our plan as a "Covered Service," they never mention their "absolute" right to deny coverage for this cutting-edge care whenever they choose – one definition for coverage when they sell their plan, and another when it comes to actually providing the care we need.

A "Worthless" Plan Description

Whether we get health insurance from our employer or purchase it directly from a healthcare insurance company, we are certain to receive an attractive brochure for the specific purpose of explaining the plan and listing what the plan provides in the way of coverage for the various forms of healthcare. Coverage that is typically displayed in a complex table of 80 percent for this, 70 percent for that, no more than 50 percent for another, and so on. Co-pays, deductibles and co-insurance are then laid on top of these varying percentages to form a plan that effectively defies an understandable comparison with other plans. Now, I really hope we have reached a point where claiming this brochure is anything but hogwash isn't necessary. Because, we should be able to agree by now that the coverage we are ACTUALLY owed is found in the insurer's signed and enforceable Provider Agreement. However, as true as that may be, our insurer wants us believe that their glossy brochure listing the various coverages from a plan is the absolute authority for what the plan will pay for the healthcare we receive.

Now, I really have to ask, doesn't the healthcare insurance

Typical Sales Contract

Sales Contract

*Product &
Payment
Requirements*

A Signed
&
Binding
Contract

Provider Agreement

Product & Payment Requirements

A Signed & Binding Contract

HMO

PPO

HDHP

POS

Plan Brochures

Non-Binding Brochures

industry have any shame? Are they so far in the tank of power and big money that truth has become an anathema to delivering the care and coverage we are owed? Has greed become such a mainstay of the healthcare insurance industry that they can routinely lie to the American people? After all, insurers know their Provider Agreements require 100 percent coverage for all the healthcare our doctor decides we need, because they wrote the damn Provider Agreements. The only question these Provider Agreements allow is whether the insurer pays for the care we need, or they contractually require the provider to pay for it.

Consequently, there can only be one answer here. The insurance industry's glossy brochures have just one purpose, i.e., to deliberately mislead you and me into believing we are owed no more than what their glossy brochure claims as the maximum the "PLAN" is required to pay for the healthcare we receive. While completely ignoring the contractual requirement that we receive all the care "our" doctor prescribes as necessary healthcare at the provider's expense.

However, even the logic of our insurer's listed coverages collapses if we apply a little simple math and reason to the percentages listed in their glossy brochure for the various forms of healthcare. Because, a figure of say 70 percent, can only have meaning if we know what the 70 percent is based on. Which can only be the discounted pricing we are entitled to receive under the terms of the Provider Agreement that our insurer has negotiated with every in-network provider. Discounted pricing that our insurer is "required" to file with the insurance department of the state we live in. But, discounted pricing that our insurer will "NOT" disclose, and contractually bars their in-network providers from even discussing with us. So, the mathematical "reality" of the percentages listed in the insurance industry's glossy brochure is that they are deliberately "UNDEFINED" and pure hogwash. Because, there is absolutely "NO" way on God's green earth for you or me to apply them to an actual in-network healthcare bill – "NO" way to check the accuracy of a bill as the CFPB is advising us to do.

The bottom line is that the insurance industry's glossy brochures claiming to define the coverage we are owed from a plan are as "worthless" as they can be, and intended to only support the insurer's freedom to pay as little as they want, whenever they want, and pass what hasn't been paid onto you and me via the American Healthcare System's "Big Lie!"

Hidden "Pricing"

We are all aware of the years of back and forth squabbling in Washington over ways to reduce the national cost of healthcare. A back and forth between Republicans and Democrats that has made it impossible to point to an argument that is particularly persuasive. However, there is an argument that we hear time and again. It's the call for greater competition in the American Healthcare System. The gist of the argument being that with greater competition comes lower prices, and with lower prices comes a stronger more accessible healthcare system. And, in truth, it's an argument that has driven the American economy and proven itself time and again. However, just for fun, let's take a closer look.

Probably the best example of what competition can do to lower price is the great American phenomenon known as "Black Friday." In fact, one only needs to mention "Black Friday" for every reader to recognize that it's the one day of the year when prices are driven below any other time of the year to create record sales. A day when American shoppers can scan the ads to find the lowest possible price for a flat screen TV, or some other prized item, and then rush out to get that sweet deal. In fact, one can argue Black Friday is the epitome of lowering price through competition.

But, what would happen if someone were to pass a rule or law that the price of an item could no longer be included in an advertisement for Black Friday? What would happen to Black Friday if the price of that flat screen TV, or other prized item, could only appear when we went to pay for it at checkout. And, even then, we found that the individual price for the item was so buried in a "Total Owed" that we couldn't identify what we were actually paying for the TV? - - - What would happen to our incentive to run out and buy that 60-inch flat screen TV? What would happen to the Black Friday phenomenon? - - - They would cease to exist.

That is exactly where our managed-care health insurance system insists we stay while our politicians call for ever greater competition. Competition on price that the American Healthcare System will not allow us to see. In fact, the American Healthcare System and the healthcare insurance industry have built an impenetrable wall between us and the prices we pay for healthcare.

Compare that with Medicare and Medicaid where prices are readily available on a government website. But, not so for the private health insurance that we get from our employer or purchase directly from an insurance company. These prices (prices which our private insurance entitles us to receive), are not only hidden from us, but the in-network providers that render the healthcare we receive and have direct access to these prices, are contractually barred from "EVER" disclosing them to us.

The bottom line here is that if our politicians are going to call for greater competition in healthcare, they need to be honest enough to acknowledge that the American Healthcare Market is a completely inelastic system, i.e., a system where price has been shown to have zero effect on the demand for healthcare services. In other words, not only does the American Healthcare System contractually bar the sharing of healthcare pricing, but the studies on pricing have shown that pricing really isn't a consideration when we need healthcare.

So please tell me, are we really going to believe that an individual seriously ill in a hospital is going to engage in price-shopping? Furthermore, we largely go to the hospital nearest our home, and, the idea that we can get a fixed price prior to entering the hospital for a serious healthcare problem is ridiculous.

The point that I am trying to make is that competition based on price demands that the pricing be open and obvious, not the deliberately hidden pricing of the American Healthcare System.

Restrictions on "Emergency" Care

Several years ago I awoke from a deep sleep to find my wife laboring for breath and in serious trouble. Because it was the middle of the night, I rushed her to the emergency room at the nearest hospital, only to again be confronted by the details of our health insurance that were never disclosed.

Because we had three separate overlapping healthcare plans, I wasn't the least bit concerned about the cost of my wife's care. I just assumed the emergency care promised by our multiple plans, and the duty the doctor owed us, would have us all on the same page. However, I couldn't have been more mistaken. Contrary to what our insurance promoted in the way of available emergency care, the reality we experienced was very different.

What you and I are not told by our insurer is that when we receive emergency care at an in-network hospital, the hospital is required to assign a single billing code that defines the emergency. Seems simple and reasonable enough, right? However, this is a code that determines exactly how much the hospital will be paid for the care we receive, regardless of whether it takes a day or a hundred days to treat us. That's right, one price regardless of how long it takes to "successfully" treat us. One price designed to limit the care you and I can get in an emergency room prior to being sent back out the door to pursue whatever other or additional care we might need – or one price to Treat-em and Street-em!

While this one-code one-price may be a policy primarily driven by insurance companies to limit what they have to pay for emergency room care, it's also a policy that meets the needs of a hospital, because emergency room care is by far the most expensive form of care a hospital can provide. Consequently, hospitals are all too willing to support the one-code one-price policy along with a Treat-em and Street-em approach to care delivered through a hospital emergency room.

The result is that hospitals and their emergency room doctors have become experts at classifying an emergency as one they can quickly remedy (better stated as "stabilize") and provide a quick discharge with a recommendation to see an outside doctor for any follow-up care that might be required.

Say, for example, you enter a hospital emergency room suffering from severe stomach cancer. You might reasonably expect that the code assigned to the emergency would be for stomach cancer. I trust you won't be too surprised to learn that isn't very likely to happen. Instead, you will almost certainly be admitted for gastrointestinal discomfort, stabilized to reduce the pain, and then discharged back to the street with the advice to *"See your doctor."*

In the case of my wife, I realized something was wrong and demanded the emergency be defined as a life-threatening condition that required she be formally admitted to the hospital. Up to that point, the emergency room doctor was saying they *simply needed to keep her in the emergency room overnight for observation. I said "No way." You are going to formally admit her to the hospital."* At which point, the doctor actually said, *"Once bitten twice shy — you know the system don't you."* I replied, *"Yes I do."* My wife was then formally admitted to the hospital, which ensured we would get the coverage we were owed.

The point I want to make here is that, had I not insisted on my wife being formally admitted to the hospital, she would have remained in the emergency room under the hospital's one-code one-price system. Which would have resulted in the cost of her care for the over-night stay being left entirely for me to pay, as her care would have been declared an uncovered benefit and the bill sent to me. A very big bill!

Once again the "Big Lie" in the American Healthcare System raises its ugly head and where we would least expect it. By keeping my wife in the emergency beyond the scope of the original emergency single billing code, the hospital would have been free to bill considerably more for her care, but outside the pricing limitations contained in the hospital's Provider Agreement. And, having exceeded those limitations, our insurer would have been free to deny coverage and allow the hospital to send us a much bigger bill. Just another example of the American Healthcare System operating at its very finest.

So, Yes. The "Big Lie" is alive and well even in nation's the emergency rooms. But, only for those who don't take the time to understand it and push back. Had I not anticipated the actions of the emergency room doctor, I have no doubt what would have happened. Not that my wife wouldn't have gotten the care she needed, at least at that particular moment. But, that the emergency room would have run-up the bill and then looked solely to us for payment. In fact, the emergency room doctor left no room for any other conclusion when he said, *"Once bitten twice shy. - You know the system don't you."*

Yes I knew the system and we were able to escape the larger bill that the hospital clearly intended to dump on us as an unsuspecting patient. But, what alarmed me more, was how cavalier the doctor was in attempting to run up the bill and pass it on to us outside our insurance.

So, should you find yourself or a loved one in an emergency room, ask to see the results of their diagnosis and whether a doctor has signed it. Insist that their attending doctor sign an "order" for discharge, not some simply worded statement where a doctor agrees to "not" object to you discharging yourself. Furthermore, "NEVER" allow an emergency room to keep you overnight for observation without being formally admitted to the hospital.

All-too-Real "Rationing"

We all know that the healthcare insurance industry **"rigorously"** denies rationing healthcare. These denials are far too wide and loud to go unheard. However, how can these denials be true when the U. S. Supreme Court has unanimously ruled that the *"inducement to ration care is the very point"* of private health insurance (Justice David H. Souter, U. S. Supreme Court in Pegram et al. v. Herdrich)? - - - They can't! But, then, who's going to stop the insurance industry from making the claim?

More to the point, since the Supreme Court has the final say on whether rationing exists in our health insurance under our system of law, the healthcare insurance industry and the American Healthcare System can only be lying when they say they aren't rationing healthcare. Lying to ensure that the "rationing" the U. S. Supreme Court says is so clearly a part of our health insurance is never acknowledged. And, lying about an issue that can literally snatch life itself from us. Worse yet, it's a lie that goes to the very core of the "Big Lie" in the American Healthcare System and has the active support of Congress.

Yes, those supporting the "Big Lie" and the need to ration healthcare will argue it's for the common good, i.e., the good of the nation. Because it cuts the national cost of healthcare. But, how can that marry with the Law when the Law is built on the rights of the individual? How can we be guaranteed Life, Liberty and the Pursuit of Happiness, along with freedom itself, when our health insurance and the American Healthcare System are given the authority to decide who can get lifesaving healthcare, and then lie about doing it? And, don't tell me this is an over-statement, because my first wife Sandy died from just such a denial (rationing) of life-saving healthcare. The recorded deci-sion of our insurer was in cold hard print. Namely, that *"given her age, the cost of the care prescribed by her doctor wasn't war-ranted."* She was 56.

What makes the lie on rationing so egregious is not so much that they do it, but how they do it. **They ration care by con-tractually barring "ALL" payment for care that an insurer refuses to cover.** Let me repeat this simple fact, because if you understand this statement, you've captured the heart of the "Big Lie" and the book. **They ration care by contractually barring "ALL" in-network payment for care your insurer refuses to cover and/or pay for.** The flip side of this rationing scheme is that an in-network provider can't bill us or accept any compen-sation for the care our insurer is refusing to approve, even if we are ready, willing and able to pay for it out of our own pocket. Which is exactly how Sandy died.

Stating this scheme as simply as I can, our insurer contrac-tually bars the in-network provider from receiving "ANY" pay-ment for care the insurer refuses to approve and/or cover. And, in so doing, RATIONS the care we are ALLOWED to receive in order to escape both the cost and the liability for the care the insurer is blocking. After all, what provider is going to render an expensive course of treatment when they know that their Pro-vider Agreement bars them from receiving "ANY" compensation for providing the care?

In short, our insurer doesn't actually deny care, they simply deny coverage. But, in so doing, they contractually bar "ALL" pay-ment for the care our doctor says we need. Consequently, the in-network doctor and hospital are told in advance that they can't get paid if they provide the care our insurer is denying for coverage. Referring to the language in a typical Provider Agreement, the provider can't ***"bill either the insurer or the enrollee"*** when coverage is denied.

But, wait. Someone in the System is surely going to argue that the bar on payment only extends to in-network providers. So, we are completely free to go outside of network for any care our insurer is refusing to cover. But, how are we supposed to know that when it's "NEVER" explained to us. How can we be expected to know that we can escape the rationing in the System by getting our healthcare outside of network? Particularly, when the Provider Agreements that are responsible for the rationing, bar anyone in the System from disclosing what is taking place.

However, this bar on payment isn't the end of their rationing scheme. The Provider Agreements that bar a provider from receiving any compensation whenever the insurer denies coverage go so far as to contractually require the doctor, hospital or other in-network provider to actually **"PROVIDE"** this denied necessary healthcare for free. That's right, you haven't misread anything. The care has to be provided for **"FREE!"**

Now, can there be any surprise that you haven't heard about the rationing in the American Healthcare System and your ability to get free healthcare whenever the System rations the care you or a loved-one need? More specifically, you aren't going to hear about it because: 1.) Your insurer's Provider Agreements absolutely bar any disclosure of the terms and conditions in these Agreements, and 2.) Disclosure of these Agreements would open in-network providers to substantial liability anytime they fail to provide necessary healthcare that an insurer is refusing to cover.

But, wait a minute the System is going to argue that you and I can always get all the healthcare we need from a non-network or out-of-network hospital. Unfortunately, only 6 percent of insured individuals get their healthcare out-of-network. So, what is the likelihood that we just might find ourselves in an out-of-network hospital when we need lifesaving healthcare? And, who is going to be shopping hospitals when we need lifesaving healthcare? No one!

The legal side of my brain just has to make the following

points: 1.) The bar on payment is a state regulatory requirement that has to be included in every Provider Agreement (although insurers have added another five or so similar provisions in these Agreements to guarantee their ability to ration the care we receive), 2.) Every Provider Agreement is reviewed by state government to ensure the bar on billing is in the Agreement, and 3.) The bar clearly <u>infringes the right of an individual to access necessary healthcare at their own expense</u>. Hence, these multiple and secret bars on billing an individual for necessary healthcare outside any participation by an insurance company are clearly an infringement on one's right to self-pay for necessary healthcare and as blatantly unconstitutional as one can get. So, can we really be surprised that the American Healthcare System and the healthcare insurance industry are so focused on keeping their Provider Agreements and rationing such a deep dark secret?

The simple truth is that the American Healthcare System, and the healthcare insurance industry, are never going to allow the disclosure of their Provider Agreements, even though the agreements: 1.) Control every aspect of the healthcare that the vast majority of the American public is both allowed to receive and forced to pay for, and 2.) The public has every right to see them as a third party beneficiary of the Agreements. That's because disclosure of these Agreements would strip them of their freedom to rationing healthcare. But even more importantly, it would close the door on their freedom to grow their bottom line.

The unfortunate truth is that healthcare insurance industry can't allow the disclosure of their Provider Agreements without striping themselves of the ability to ration healthcare and grow their bottom line. After all, what other American industry can add to its profits by simply refusing to pay its suppliers, i.e., refusing to pay it's bills?

So, you and I can be absolutely certain that there isn't going to be any meaningful discussion of the rationing that is so rampant within the American Healthcare System. In fact, the only choice we can be assured of is whether to stand idly by and suffer the consequences of the System's rationing, or educate ourselves on the care and coverage we are "ACTUALLY" owed from our health insurance.

We need to be more "up front in talking to patients about rationing" (Dr. Steven D. Pearson, Harvard Medical School).

Their "Secret" Provider Agreements

As fixated as the American Healthcare System is on avoiding any discussion of rationing, it has been more than willing to argue that rationing would be the certain outcome if the federal government were to provide universal health insurance. The underlying message being that private health insurance <u>does not ration healthcare</u> and universal government health insurance would. However, we now know that rationing is exactly what our private health insurance is doing, and we have the U. S. Supreme Court to thank for confirming it. So, how can the private insurance industry and our plan live in these two completely opposite worlds? How can our health insurance have the Supreme Court rule that rationing is the *"very point"* of their business model, and yet feel completely free to promote the very opposite? How can the private healthcare insurance industry make rationing *"the very point"* of their plans, but keep it outside the view of the press, the public, and yes, you and me? - - - HOW?

They do it by establishing "secret" contracts (Provider Agreements) with every in-network doctor, hospital, and other provider of healthcare services and products. <u>And, then they lie!</u> All the while ensuring that their Provider Agreements remain a deep dark secret.

For those who would question my emphasis on the intentional "secrecy" of these Provider Agreements, please consider the following references. And, please understand that these Provider Agreements have been in existence and have remained essentially unchanged for something like 30 years.

Congressional Research Service, 1997

The Congressional Research Service's report for Congress entitled "Managed Health Care: Federal and State Regulation," issued in 1997, is more than thirty pages long. Yet it states only that the *"contracts between an HMO and a participating provider be in writing"* and that *"The HMO must ensure that in the event that it fails to pay for services, the subscriber or enrollee is not liable to the provider for any amounts owed by the HMO."* **The "VERY" point of the book.** However, the Report provides no further explanation of a provision in state-mandated Provider Agreements that any first-year law student would recognize raises all kinds of questions and issues. Particularly if we have an HMO plan and get billed for what our doctor has determined is the healthcare we need.

Congressional Research Service, 2010
A second Congressional Research Service report in 2010 entitled "The Market Structure of the Health Insurance Industry" is more than sixty pages long. Yet it makes absolutely no mention of these state-mandated Provider Agreements that the earlier Congressional Report acknowledged form the contractual relationship between in-network providers and insurers and severely limit what an in-network provider can bill for healthcare. Once again, any first year law student will recognize that this absence can only be by design. Think about it. The U. S. Supreme Court has ruled that the *"inducement to ration care is the very point"* of our private health insurance, yet the 2010 Report to Congress makes no mention of the Provider Agreements that make this rationing possible.

NAIC HMO Model Act, revised July 2005
To this point, you have only had my claim and reasoning that the insurance industry's Provider Agreements are a well-kept secret. However, the NAIC HMO Model Act of 2005 removes all doubt as to whether the Agreements are being deliberately hidden from the public. The Act literally states that the insurance industry's Provider Agreements shall be treated as *"trade secrets,"* which means that the states are to use their power to keep you and me from ever seeing them.

It's important to understand that under our form of government, the states have the primary responsibility for overseeing healthcare and insurance, not the Federal Government. And, the NAIC (the National Association of Insurance Commissioners) is an organization that is: 1.) Comprised of the heads of the state agencies responsible for providing this oversight, and 2.) Developing a unified approach to the healthcare insurance market. So when the NAIC says the insurance industry's Provider Agreements are to be treated as *"trade Secrets,"* it is speaking for the very people with the authority and "power" to ensure that these Provider Agreements are kept secret.

The American Medical Association, 2005

The AMA's "Model Managed Care Contract" (Provider Agreement), published in 2005, is sixty-seven pages long and intended to both explain and recommend what a doctor should consider before signing a Provider Agreement. However, section 3.11 of this "Model Contract," a section entitled "Sole Source of Payment," states that *"Where Enrollee is enrolled in a Plan subject to state or federal legal requirements that prohibit a physician from billing patients for Covered Services in the event that the Payer"* (the insurer) *"fails to make such payment, the Medical Services Entity"* (doctor, hospital, or other healthcare provider) *"agrees to look solely to that Payer"* (again the insurer) *"for payment of all Covered Services delivered during the terms of the Agreement."* Consequently, we have the AMA just accepting the fact that their membership "CANNOT" BILL you or me for any necessary healthcare when our insurer or plan fails to pay for it. Yet, the AMA offers absolutely no explanation of how these contractual restraints comply with the law or how they can be explained or justified.

This absence of any AMA-proposed alternative language or explanation of how a doctor might privately contract for the care an insurer is refusing to approve for coverage is mind-blowing. Particularly, when the AMA, in another section of its Model Contract entitled "Medical Necessity and Due Process," states that *"Generally speaking, managed care organizations"* (our insurer) *"will pay for Covered Services that are medically necessary."* How much clearer can it get? The AMA is acknowledging, in simple English, that there will be times when an insurer will refuse to pay for necessary healthcare and the doctor will have to absorb the cost. Even more to the point, the AMA provides absolutely "NO" recourse for a doctor who has been placed in the position of having to absorb the cost of an insurer's failure to pay for the healthcare we need.

ERISA Preemption Manual for State Health Policy Makers

In its more than 110-page policy manual, the National Academy for State Health Policy devotes a mere two sentences to the state-mandated provisions in a Provider Agreement.- - - It states that the terms of these Provider Agreements *"prohibit providers from seeking remuneration from enrollees if the plan fails to pay."* And, *"States may want to require that these provider hold-harmless guarantees be part of plan-enrollee contracts in order to better defend them as insurance regulation."* Two statements that: 1.) Confirm the message of the book, and 2.) Acknowledge the means of rationing used by healthcare insurance companies is most likely indefensible. - - - So, can it be any surprise that these Provider Agreements are such a well-kept secret?

While the ERISA Preemption Manual may advocate *"that these provider hold-harmless guarantees be part of plan-enrollee contracts in order to better defend them as insurance regulation,"* this has "NEVER" been done. And, I can assure you that it will "NEVER" be done. Because, to adopt this recommended change would require the introduction of individual contracts/policies similar to what is required for all the other forms of real insurance in our life. And, that can only be done through substantial regulatory change that would demand opening the entire issue of "rationing" to public review and comment. Even more problematic is that the change would have the potential of gutting the insurance industry's current business model and opening the industry's scheme of rationing and the "Big Lie" to review by the court.

No, the only way forward for the Healthcare Insurance Industry and the American Healthcare System is to keep their Provider Agreements locked away and as far from the public as possible. Locked away from any discussion of the industry's claim of never denying care, and certainly never rationing care. All made possible by Provider Agreements that you and I are not allowed to see.

The "Enrollee Hold Harmless" Clause

For those who might believe they can always pay for the healthcare they **"NEED"** if their insurer refuses coverage, you need to read the following language taken directly from a typical Provider Agreement. And, remember, every in-network provider you go to will have signed such an Agreement with language similar to what's shown below. Furthermore, you need to understand that Non-Covered Services are defined as only those services that are **"NOT"** medically necessary. So if you need a face lift, you are free to go for it. You can not only pay for it, you will have to pay for it because it will be classified as a Non-Covered Service right from the get-go. But, if you need reconstructive heart surgery, and your plan denies coverage for whatever reason, good luck getting it. Because your plan won't pay for it and you won't be allowed to pay for it either. The following contractual language just can't be read any other way.

> **Provider agrees that in no event, including but not limited to non-payment by Insurance Company, Insurance Company's insolvency or breach of this agreement, shall Provider, one of its subcontractors, or any of its employees or independent contractors bill, charge, collect a deposit from, seek compensation, remuneration or reimbursement from, or have any recourse against an Enrollee or persons other than the insurance company acting on behalf of Enrollee for Covered Services provided pursuant to this Agreement. This provision shall not prohibit the collection of coinsurance, co-payments or charges for Non-Covered Services. Provider further agrees that (1) this provision shall survive the termination of this Agreement regardless of the cause giving rise to termination and shall be construed to be for the benefit of the Enrollees, and that (2) this provision supersedes any oral or written contrary agreement now existing or hereafter entered into between Provider and Enrollees or persons acting on their behalf. Provider may not change, amend or waive this provision without prior written consent of the Insurance Company. Any attempt to change, amend or waive this provision are void.**

In a world where no two attorneys ever use the exact same language for a similar contractual provision, and no two states ever use the same language for a similar piece of legislation, the insurance industry's Enrollee Hold Harmless clause stands out as a bold exception. Quietly imbedded in the laws of every state where it's mandated for incorporation in every in-network Provider Agreement, the Enrollee Hold Harmless clause has been included in millions of Provider Agreements with no explanation or disclosure.

Much as the Greeks decorated their Trojan horse to ensure the people of Troy wouldn't look inside, the states and the insurance industry have adorned their Enrollee Hold Harmless clause with the claim that it's been enacted solely for the benefit of those with health insurance. But, where the Greeks merely encouraged the people of Troy to not look inside, the insurance industry and the American Healthcare System have done them one better. They have locked the door to ensure that no one gets to look inside the clause. And, per the NAIC, we are to simply accept the fact that the clause, along with its Provider Agreement, are to be treated as a *"trade secret."*

Just as the people of Troy stood idly by as that ancient wooden horse was pulled within their city walls, we have been <u>forced</u> to stand idly by as the Enrollee Hold Harmless clause has been incorporated into every in-network Provider Agreement in the country. Yet, I have never found a single person or organization questioning its purpose or, more particularly, the reach of its language. And, in my many years researching the workings of the American Healthcare System, I have never found a single person willing and able to discuss the provisions that are incorporated in these Provider Agreements.

In fact, I haven't even been able to find a record or report of the legislative process that was used by the states to enact the Clause. Absolutely nothing, even though the Clause: 1.) Leaves no ability to pay for "necessary and appropriate" health care other than what an insurer is willing to cover, 2.) Bars physicians from receiving any pay whatsoever unless they accept the medical decisions of an insurer, and 3.) Severs the doctor-patient relationship in terms of who is actually deciding the healthcare we need.

Originally drafted by NAIC, the Enrollee Hold Harmless clause has become a part of the laws and regulations of every state in the country (a finding of the *Study of Balanced Billing Prohibitions in Maryland,* 2002). Specifically, these laws and regulations require HMOs to have a written state-approved Provider Agreement with every doctor, hospital, and other provider of health care services within their network of approved providers, and that the Agreement <u>contain the Enrollee Hold Harmless clause</u>. In fact, it's impossible to gage the reach of the Clause, because the states have allowed insurers to establish a single Provider Agreement that covers all their many types of plans, as well as extends to all their subsidiaries, affiliates, contractors, subcontractors, and who knows how many others. Thus, the states have allowed healthcare insurance companies to become the sole judge and jury of the healthcare we need and should be allowed to receive, i.e., a judge and jury with no <u>liability</u> for the quality, appropriateness, or the outcome of the care they allow us to receive.

Fortunately, you don't have to rely on my analysis of the Clause or the book. On October 18, 2022 Blue Cross Blue Shield of North Carolina was kind enough to publish the exact point I am making. ***"The participating provider - - - must write-off the cost of the non-certified or noncovered services and hold the member financially harmless."***

No, the insurance industry's Provider Agreements, along with their Hold Harmless clause and several other provisions, don't say we can't get the care we need. In fact these Agreements specifically state that the in-network provider must provide all "Medically Necessary" healthcare that can only be determined by "OUR" doctor, and not the insurer or the insurer's doctor. However, it then bars all payment for the care "UNLESS" the insurer chooses to cover the cost.

"We have tried everything, and there is just no way under the Enrollee Hold Harmless clause for an enrollee to pay for necessary health care." **David Murdock, former Vice President of Legal for the Caron Foundation.**

David Murdock recounted years of trying to find a way around the Clause and failing. However, the typical Provider Agreement contains at least five other provisions that prevent a provider from billing for care that an insurer has refused to cover. So, even if David Murdock had found a way around the Enrollee Hold Harmless clause, he would have run smack into other provisions that would have stopped him dead in his tracks.

A great example of these other provisions is the Utilization Review provision that allows an insurer to reverse an earlier decision on coverage and then claw back any money paid out as coverage. And, please note that this Utilization Review provision specifically states that a patient can't be billed to recover the money being clawed back. Again, not something we are likely to be told when a provider passes the cost of one of these reversals of coverage on to us.

The fact that the Enrollee Hold Harmless clause bars all compensation for a provider when your insurer denies coverage is clearly stated in the language of the clause. However, I can assure you that your state will twist its self into a pretzel to claim otherwise. All the while refusing to allow you to read the Provider Agreement at issue.

Under Supreme Court rulings, a state has the power to interpret the language it uses in its legislation and law. However, that authority only extends to a state's enforcement of its own legislation and law. Here, the state is: 1.) Requiring that the clause is included in a private contract between two private parties, and 2.) Only requiring that the language be "similar" to the draft provided by the state. This takes the interpretation of the clause completely out from under a state's discretion to enforce, and subjects it solely to a four-corner analysis of an agreement between two private parties under contract law. All legal BS for your state trying to mislead you and keep you as far away from your insurer's Provider Agreement with its inherent rationing as possible.

There's one last point worth making to show just how willing the states are to mislead you and me when it comes to rationing our healthcare. If we go back to the language shown above for the Enrollee Hold Harmless clause, we find the state insisting that *"This provision shall not prohibit the collection of coin-surance, co-payments or charges for Non-Covered Services."* Now, I am not going to claim to be any great authority on mathematics. However, even I can see the ridiculousness of the states' claim that the **collection of coinsurance, co-payments** is unaffected by the Enrollee Hold Harmless clause. Because, if there isn't any allowable "BILLING" for denied coverage, there can't be any *coinsurance* or *co-payments*, period! It's a mathematical impossibility, because both are determined as some percentage or part of an allowable billing. Furthermore, a *Non-Covered Service* falls completely outside the terms of a Provider Agreement and has to be billed to you and me if a provider wants to get paid.

No Help "Available"

One thing that should be clear by now is that the healthcare insurance industry isn't led by dummies. They are very smart people dedicated to keeping the money pouring in. But, this shouldn't come as any surprise because every for-profit business in the country has this very same mantra. In fact, this isn't even meant as a criticism, because it's a simple statement of fact.

However, not content with the advantage that Enrollee Hold Harmless clause and five or so other provisions in a Provider Agreement that allow insurers to ration healthcare and drive profits, the insurance industry is working hard to move employer based health insurance out from under the laws specifically enacted to ensure these plans deliver the care and coverage they owe their enrollees. Let me say that again. Insurers are moving their "plans" out from under the oversight that was created to ensure we get what we are owed. The result is that by the end of 2022, more than 60 percent of those who get their health insurance from an employer are now without anyone to call when their plan fails to provide the care and coverage they are owed.

Deliberately outside the view of the public, employment-based health insurance is being split into two very different categories: fully insured plans on one hand, and self-funded plans on the other. The distinction between the two being whether an employer has chosen to: 1.) Purchased a plan that covers the cost of their employee's healthcare (the form of insurance that has been the standard in the U.S. for more than fifty years), or 2.) Uses its own funds to cover those healthcare costs and have an insurance company simply administer the plan.

Stating the difference again, but with slightly simpler wording, the fully *"insured plan"* is one where the insurer owns the plan and the employer simply pays an admission fee to have its employees admitted to the insurer's plan. A *"self-funded plan"* is where the employer owns the plan and an insurance company is hired to simply administer the employer's plan.

It all sounds so trivial, right? Because, in both cases an insurer is administering the plan so the care and coverage should be the same. The only obvious difference is where the money is coming from to pay for an employee's healthcare. So, it's just a trivial change in funding you might say. However - - -

My wife and I own a business with roughly 50 employees. Two years ago, we got a request from our insurer to convert to a self-funded plan. We then got a 17-page contract of fine print to define the plan. Print so fine and complex that it took me five readings to reach a point where I felt I understood it. Five readings to understand that the contract required our company to grant the insurer full control over all healthcare decisions, but for our business to accept the liable for those decisions. In short, the insurer was to get the ability to decide the healthcare our employees would be allowed to receive, while we alone would shoulder the liability for those decisions, because it was "our" plan.

Now, I hope you won't be too surprised to hear we never signed that contract. Furthermore, we never even got a response when I formally questioned the fine print that assigned us the liability for the decisions that the insurer would be making.

Unfortunately, our example is only a small part of a major effort on the part of the insurance industry to move further and further away from what we have been led to view as an insurance product. And, in so doing, escape any meaningful oversight or liability for their actions in rationing healthcare. It's a movement that has been ever-so-subtle and undiscussed that an employee isn't likely to even know what kind of a plan he or she has. And, I can pretty much guarantee that an employer isn't about to explain the change – a change where the two types of insurance use the very same insurance card. So, it's very unlikely that an employee will even know to question the type of plan he or she has.

In fact, the only time the difference between these two types of plans is likely to bubble to the surface is if we need help in getting the care and coverage we are owed from our plan.

However, this is where the rubber meets the road. Because, if we have a self-funded plan, we are going to find there won't be anyone to call for help. What would appear to be little more than a shift in funding, actually moves the plan out from under the state regulation and oversight that was designed and staffed to ensure we get the care and coverage we are owed, i.e., someone to answer the phone when we go looking for help.

Yes, later in the book I will be quite critical of the support the states provide the insurance industry. But, a large part of this book is based on the regulation and oversight that the states provide to guarantee us our own doctor and access to quality healthcare.

However, with what would appear to be nothing more than a mere shift in funding, the insurance industry has been able to put all that regulation and oversight in the rear view mirror. They have moved sixty percent of all those with employer sup-plied health insurance out from under state regulation and slid these plans in under in under <u>Federal regulation and oversight that essentially does "not" exist</u>. Federal regulation and over-sight that essentially cannot exist because the states have been assigned that role under the separation of powers and the U. S. Constitution.

This is just another part of the plan your insurer won't dis-close, and the plan they deliberately "Hide." And, why wouldn't they? After all, it's once again a clear win for everyone but us. Insurers get to move their plans out from under regulation and oversight (essentially eliminating the need to comply with the Affordable Care Act (Obama Care) and "ALL" consumer protec-tion laws). Employers get a less expensive plan. And, Congress gets the rationing that the Supreme Court has ruled is an essential part of the American Healthcare System. And **"nobody"** is accountable but us. God, these guys are good!

Which all translates to millions of Americans being secretly placed outside the laws that were specifically created to: 1.) Guarantee we get the care and coverage we are owed, 2.) Ban the practice of surprise billing and 3.) Provide the help and enforcement we need when our plan fails to provide the care and coverage we are owed.

In short, not only has the healthcare insurance industry found a way to put its rationing outside the reach of any reasonable liability and the law, but they have simultaneously found a way to ensure there is no one to answer the phone if we get so bold as to ask for help in getting what we are owed, i.e., **"no help available."**

HMO, PPO or HDHP it "Doesn't" Matter

When I first became aware of just how easy it is for an insurer to deny care and coverage, the predominant plan in the country was the HMO. And, by the time I had written two books on the subject, the PPO was fast approaching the dominance originally held by the HMO. Today, the two are close to equal in their share of the market, with HDHPs (High Deductible Healthcare Plan) rapidly growing in popularity. But, these aren't the only plans out there. Each of the acronyms cited offers a range of individual plans within the category. In addition, there are 1096 healthcare insurance companies registered with the NAIC (the last time I checked), and more than 5000 registered in the country. In essence, the array of plans in the U.S. market is nothing less than mind-blowing. Each with its own mind-numbing array of deductibles, co-pays, coinsurance and differing levels of coverage for the countless types of healthcare. So, what do all these various plans and supposed differences mean to you and me? How different are they in terms of the care and coverage they provide?

Fortunately, there is a simple answer, because every plan points to a "contract" that defines the coverage it provides. But wait a minute, what contract are they talking about? There is

"NO" contract or policy that one would expect when purchasing insurance. Or, for that matter, when purchasing anything that requires a contract to nail down what we are owed.

Once again, the American Healthcare System raises its ugly head. The contract that the healthcare insurance industry cites for defining the care and coverage we are owed from a healthcare plan is bogus and deliberately misleading. You can't get blood from a stone, and you certainly can't get a definition for the care and coverage we are owed from a contract that doesn't exist.

As we have stressed and continue to stress, the only contracts that "do" exist in the American Healthcare System are the insurance industry's Provider Agreements. One Agreement covering all of an insurer's many plans – HMO, PPO, HDHP or whatever an insurer chooses to call a particular plan. And, one Agreement that defines what we are owed in care and coverage, as well as <u>exactly who, when and what an in-network provider can bill</u>. One Agreement regardless of the number or types of plans an insurer markets or the number of times an insurer revises its plans – one Agreement guaranteeing all the necessary healthcare you and I need!

But, if there are some 5000 healthcare insurance companies, how can they create all the required Provider Agreements? - - - The truth is that they can't! Only the very largest insurers can afford to establish a network of contracted and state approved in-network providers. The rest of the some 5000 insurance companies simply pay one of these large insurers to use their network. Which brings us back to their being only "ONE" Provider Agreement that defines the care and coverage we are owed.

This is a hugely important point because it strips away all the BS the insurance industry and the American Healthcare System want us to believe so they can ration our healthcare and promote the "BIG Lie." All translating to there being no practical difference between the insurance industries' many acronyms, plans and whatever's. Consequently, as long as we stay in-network, HMO, PPO, HDHP, revised plan, or whatever an insurer chooses to call its plan, it really **"Doesn't Matter"**!

Care & Coverage "EVEN" When Your Plan Says "No"

When Justice David Souter published the U. S. Supreme Court's unanimous decision in Pegram v. Herdrich, he wrote that the *"inducement to ration care is the very point of any HMO scheme."* So one might reasonably think that the Court's decision applies only to HMOs. After all, that's exactly what Justice Souter wrote. However, we now know that the Provider Agreements that made rationing so obvious to Justice Souter and the Supreme Court are the very same Provider Agreements that insurers are using to administer all of their new and revised plans. Or more simply put, there is still just one Provider Agreement that defines an in-network provider – one Provider Agreement regardless of what an insurer chooses to call a particular plan – just one Provider Agreement to administer an ever-growing list of catchy acronyms and new plans – and, just one Provider Agreement that allowed the U. S. Supreme Court to <u>unanimously</u> conclude that the *"inducement to ration care"* is at the very core of the "scheme" insurers use when saying "NO" to the care and coverage our doctor says we need.

However, the *"inducement"* to ration healthcare is a far cry from having the authority to actually do it under U. S. Law. That's because the rationing of healthcare requires the ability to overrule the medical judgment of a properly licensed attending physician (our doctor) – a physician who the law has given the sole authority to determine necessary and appropriate healthcare. In fact, this authority is so firmly embedded in the law that it can't be changed any more than the laws governing the decision-making of a licensed engineer, an attorney, or a CPA can be changed. Furthermore, as long as there is an offer (ANY OFFER) to pay for the care our doctor prescribes as necessary healthcare, a hospital is legally required to provide the care. And, if for some reason the hospital is unable to provide it, they are legally obligated to find another hospital to provide it.

That's the law in the United States. And, it's what the American Healthcare System had to overcome in designing their *"scheme"* for rationing healthcare. A *"scheme"* that demands a backdoor approach to overruling the medical judgement of our doctor, i.e., a backdoor that circumvents the legal authority that is so clearly assigned to our doctor.

However, like most doors, the insurers' backdoor can be made to swing both ways – just as long as you and I understand how the door works and the inherent Achilles Heel in its design – an Achilles Heel we can use to swing the door the other way and effectively pull the rug out from under their rationing scheme.

Fortunately, the existence of this backdoor isn't by chance. It's by necessity. That's because insurers can't be seen breaking the law to ration healthcare. The liability that would create could put insurers out of the rationing business in a hurry. So, they need to have their rationing appear to be something else, i.e., coverage.

So, our ever-so-clever insurance industry designed their backdoor to block "PAYMENT" and not "CARE." And, while this may seem to be a very trivial point, I assure you it is no such thing. Because, this is very core of the scheme the insurance industry uses to ration healthcare, as well as the key to allowing us to swing their backdoor the other way.

Simply put, an insurer "NEVER" denies "CARE" to ration healthcare. They simply block any and all "PAYMENT" for the care they ration. Coverage is just a smokescreen to keep you and me fighting the wrong war. The real issue is "PAYMENT." Because, the industry's Provider Agreements bar every in-network provider from accepting any form "PAYMENT" for care the insurer has decided to deny and ration. And, while I hate to say it, a denial of "COVERAGE" is completely within the rights of an insurance company as unanimously determined by Justice Souter and the U. S. Supreme Court.

However, to ensure that their right to deny coverage isn't viewed as a denial of care, the insurance industry crafted their Provider Agreements to: 1.) **"REQUIRE"** in-network providers to provide all necessary healthcare regardless of how the insurer rules on coverage, 2.) **"Allow"** the insurer to deny coverage and payment whenever it chooses, and 3.) Bar **"ALL"** forms of billing for care that the insurer refuses to approve and cover.

Consequently, the insurers' backdoor to rationing doesn't rely on an ability to overrule our doctor. It merely relies on a "contractual" provision that <u>bars all forms of billing and payment whenever the insurer denies coverage for the care our doctor says we need</u>.

Now, please tell me. What doctor, hospital or other provider of in-network healthcare services is going to risk losing thousands of dollars in unpaid healthcare costs to deliver healthcare that our insurer is refusing to approve? In simple English, they aren't! Particularly, given the ease with which a provider can blame the whole mess on "OUR" inability to get the necessary coverage for the care our doctor is prescribing. Namely, it's our insurance. Therefore it's our problem. Case closed, while we plead with our insurer to provide the coverage the hospital or other in-network provider is requiring. And, the insurer is completely within its rights to refuse.

Fortunately for us, and unfortunately for the insurance industry, their backdoor "scheme" to overrule our doctor relies on complete secrecy. Because, once you and I understand what the insurer is doing, we can swing the door the other way to get the care we need, **"without having to pay for it."** We can simply demand the care our doctor is prescribing by insisting on paying for it (<u>as is our right under the law</u>), sign whatever payment agreement is required, get the care as the law demands, AND "then" simply remind the provider that they surrendered their right to bill us when they signed their Provider Agreement.

Yes, the insurance industry has once again proven itself extremely clever in constructing their *"scheme"* for rationing healthcare. Because, it's a contractual structure that you and I would never suspect <u>let alone be allowed to see</u>. However, it's a structure that opens the possibility of yet another Achilles Heel in the System's rationing *"scheme."*

When the insurance industry first wrote their Provider Agreements, HMOs were the only game in town and the sole property of an insurance company. However, that's no longer true. Employees are now being required to contribute DIRECTLY to the cost of their membership in a plan. That's right, where plans were once the sole property of an insurance company, insured individuals are now paying at least some portion of the cost of a plan. Furthermore, where a plan has been switched to a Fully Funded Plan, the employer now owns the plan, and with ownership should come some form of access to the Provider Agreements that define the plan.

In short, the game of keeping the insurance industry's Provider Agreements, along with their "scheme" for rationing healthcare, a deep dark secret has changed. Employees who were once simply given health insurance, can now claim some direct ownership in a plan. They are no longer merely third-party beneficiaries of a plan in which they had no direct ownership or contractual rights. Consequently, while keeping the insurance industry's Provider Agreements a deep dark secret might have seemed straight forward in the past, the growing practice of having employees contribute directly to the purchase of a plan changes things. Because, with ownership generally comes some right of participation – participation that can only be seen as a growing threat to the secrecy of the insurance industry's Provider Agreements. Most importantly, it provides another reason to turn a blind eye to our use of the System's backdoor to get the care and coverage we are owed.

The bottom line is that the insurance industry simply can't afford disclosure of these Provider Agreements, let alone their "scheme" for rationing healthcare, and certainly not the existence of their backdoor to the care we need. Because, it could literally gut the entire private healthcare insurance industry. So, let's be smart and use this vulnerability to our advantage. Let's use the backdoor they created to get the care and coverage our doctor says we need. And, literally "dare" the System to publically contest our use of it. Let's be smart enough to use this backdoor that could very well have saved the life of my wife Sandy.

Lastly, since the in-network provider is a contract arm of our insurer, we really shouldn't care whether our insurer or their in-network provider pays for the care our doctor has determined we need. In essence, the two are effectively one and the same under the provisions of their Provider Agreement. Consequently, we need to view coverage is coverage whether it comes from our insurer or their in-network provider. It really shouldn't make any difference. We need to see it as simply someone other than us providing the coverage we are owed and they have contractually agreed to provide.

Suggestions for When your Plan Says "No"

1.) Demand the right to pay for the care your doctor is prescribing as necessary healthcare, but your insurer is refusing to cover.

2.) Agree to sign whatever the provider wants to guarantee payment.

3.) Threaten to call the State Attorney General if the provider fails to accept your offer to pay for the care you need, because such a refusal is a violation of state law. So, you will almost certainly get the care you need!

4.) After getting the care, simply sit back and wait for the bill.

5.) Then, when the bill arrives, write across it with a big red pen, ***"This is a legally unenforceable debt per the terms of the Provider Agreement that you signed with my insurer. Consequently, please don't bother me again."*** Put the bill in an envelope and return it by registered mail to whoever sent it, along with a copy to your insurer and your employer if you get your insurance from your employer.

6.) And, the entire matter should be over. If not, go to the back of the book for suggestions on how to demand an even greater review of the bill as is your right under the provisions of the U. S. Fair Debt Collection Act.

An Unholy "Alliance" with Government

In 2020, I wrote to the Center for Medicare & Medicaid (CMS) and asked if I enrolled in a Medicare Advantage Plan, would I "still be protected by the federal Medicare Laws on billing." The answer I got in a 9/18/2020 letter (DCN: 200914L7425398) was ***"YES."*** The letter then went on to say, ***"However the Medi-***

care Advantage plans may have different rules and different out of pocket cost." And, I would *"need to get my healthcare from an in-network Provider."* All complete BS when it came to answering my question.

To be completely truthful, I had expected CMS to find a way to avoid answering my question. What I didn't expect, was for CMS to be so bold in their support of the "Big Lie."

The CMS statement of *"YES"* I would *"still be protected by the federal Medicare Laws"* is so ludicrous that it can only be seen as a deliberate lie. That's because Medicare Advantage is nothing more than "private" health insurance purchased by the federal government for those over 65 wanting something other than Medicare. In essence, Medicare Advantage plans are the very same plans you and I get from our employer, or purchase directly from an insurance company – plans defined by the same Provider Agreements that the private insurance industry keeps so carefully hidden.

So, for CMS to claim that Medicare billing protections apply to Medicare Advantage plans is equivalent to claiming they apply to all private health insurance. Laughable if it wasn't such a deliberate attempt to mislead the public. After-all, Medicare actually "bars" billing us when coverage is denied for the care we receive.

That being said, we really need to ask why CMS would be so blatant in their misrepresentation of the billing protections for Medicare Advantage plans? Why would CMS choose to lie rather than simply duck my question or provide some rambling legalese that skirts the issue? Why go on the record with a statement that is so obviously false?

Because, to do otherwise could very well have opened the door to a discussion of the "Big Lie." Something I hope we can agree no one in the American Healthcare System wants to allow. Furthermore, there was very little chance that I would know enough to catch their misrepresentation of these plans.

Unfortunately, there is a third reason that's actually very possible. The insurance industry has done such a great job of hiding the truth and selling the "Big Lie," that whoever in CMS answered my letter may actually have believed they were telling the truth. Sad, but in my experience, all-too real!

There is also the question of whether the letter from CMS is an anomaly, or a systemic willingness to mislead the American people. So, let's delve deeper into that issue and see if we can find an answer.

Clue #1
Our first clue to an answer comes right off the CMS website. It's their *"Partnering with Providers to promote a smoothly functioning healthcare system".* - - - They are in bed with the very people promoting the "Big Lie." So, why wouldn't they choose to mislead us in order to protect their PARTNERS in the 4-trillion dollar American Healthcare System?

Clue #2
The "Big Lie" is the private insurance industry's primary tool for controlling the cost of healthcare, i.e., the rationing of our healthcare. The same can be said for Medicare Advantage, because it's the same "private" insurance you and I get from our employer and it operates off the same Provider Agreements. Consequently, both CMS and the private healthcare insurance industry are in the business of shifting the cost of healthcare away from insurance and <u>onto you and me</u>. Which can only mean they both feel the need to feed us the "Big Lie."

Clue #3
The states religiously misrepresent the reach of the Enrollee Hold Harmless clause. Rather than acknowledge the actual language of the Clause, the states faithfully parrot a claim that it only applies in cases of insurer insolvency. However, the language clearly doesn't limit the clause to insurer insolvency. A point made earlier in the book and a point that the government attorneys at CMS have to understand.

Clue #4
In 2004, the healthcare insurance companies in Pennsylvania were refusing to cover hospitalization for drug and alcohol addiction, even though Pennsylvania Law specificity stated that the hospitalization was to be covered by insurers. These refusals become so common, that the state's Insurance Commissioner felt compelled to clarify exactly who had the final say in deter-

mining medically necessary care for drug and alcohol addiction, i.e. covered hospitalization. And, because the law specifically assigned that authority to a "licensed physician or psychologist (an individual's doctor)," the Commissioner's Notice 2003-06 said the same thing.

The insurance industry immediately sued the Pennsylvania Insurance Department claiming that the Commissioner's Notice reversed fourteen years of policy where insurers were allowed to have the final say on determining "necessary healthcare."

What makes the case so unique, is that both parties to the suit agreed the issue was purely one of the language in the law. Both sides acknowledging that the legislature had generally **"encouraged"** insurers to have the final say on necessary healthcare. So, the case boiled down to determining whether an insurer could have the final say, when this specific law assigned that authority to a properly licensed attending physician, i.e., our doctor.

The issue was "so important" that a final and laughful decision from the Court didn't come until six years later when the Pennsylvania Supreme Court very quietly ruled that: 1.) The intent of the Legislature is clear in stating that a "licensed physician is to determine "necessary healthcare," 2.) The Insurance Commissioner's 2003 Notice was simply *"a statement of policy, without binding effect"* and *"does not establish a binding norm,"* and 3.) Insurer's right to have the final say on necessary healthcare has *"been properly recognized."*

So, can it be any clearer that the state of Pennsylvania turned itself into a pretzel to bury the case and quietly walk away from a decision that could only have recognized the plain language of the Law. Furthermore, the case clearly put the Pennsylvania Insurance Department and the Court on the record agreeing to look the other way when it comes to an insurance company overruling a doctor to ration healthcare. A final say that, quite literally, took the life of my wife Sandy.

Clue #5

My fifth and last example is a statement I got from the Chair of the House Subcommittee on Health when I asked about the reach of the Enrollee Hold Harmless clause. He replied by asking *"why I should care if I can't pay for my own healthcare."* To which I replied that he had no right to take it from me, let alone to take it in secret. He then made it extremely clear I was too "bugger off" as my English relatives are fond of saying. The congressman's obvious frustration being that I had dared to point out that the language in the Clause is so absolute that it actually bars an individual from paying for their own healthcare when their insurer denies coverage.

All this, and you still can't believe that our government is knowingly supporting the "Big Lie". Well, let's delve deeper.

A number of states have modified their Enrollee Hold Harmless clause purportedly to clarify the intent of the ban on billing an enrollee when coverage is denied. For instance, on August 28, 2001, the state of Missouri altered its Enrollee Hold Harmless clause to include *"This agreement shall not prohibit the provider from collecting coinsurance, deductibles or copayments - - - or fees for uncovered services."* Meaning that Provider Agreements in Missouri would NOW allow an in-network provider to COLLECT *coinsurance, deductibles or copayments* along with *fees for uncovered services* whenever an insurer denies coverage. But wait a minute, the change specifically states "collect" these charges. It does not state that a provider can "bill" in such circumstances. Furthermore, to "collect" is not the same as to "bill." To collect is to simply accept or gather something. Where to bill is a formal declaration of one's claim against another, and, an act that is strictly forbidden by the surviving language of the state's Enrollee Hold Harmless clause, i.e., *"Provider agrees that in no event, - - - shall the provider bill - - - an enrollee."*

What we have, once again, is a state twisting itself into a pretzel to defend the Enrollee Hold Harmless clause and the rationing it creates.

Prior to the change, Missouri's Enrollee Hold Harmless clause made it virtually impossible for an in-network provider to bill an enrollee when the insurer failed to cover the cost of necessary healthcare. In fact, as I explained earlier, the V. P. of Legal for the Caron Foundation, David Murdock, had told me that the Foundation had moved heaven and earth to find a way around the bar and failed. He further explained that the bar was so absolute that a patient needing hospitalization for alcohol addiction couldn't pay for their own care when their insurer denied coverage, an all-too-common problem in Pennsylvania as I explain above. It's also a complaint I heard time and again in testimony before the Pennsylvania Legislature. Furthermore, it's the very issue that kept me in a Pennsylvania courtroom for 8-long years following the death of my wife Sandy.

But, there was a more fundamental problem with the Enrollee Hold Harmless clause. That's because there were a number of areas impacted by the clause where a state would have a hard time justifying it as an appropriate use of its authority to regulate insurance. And, just coincidently mind you, those areas were *coinsurance, deductibles or copayments and fees for uncovered services.* The logic here being that: 1.) A provider would have a right to receive these payments, and 2.) The payments would be outside the coverage of an insurance plan, and thus outside the regulation of insurance.

So, Missouri simply modified its Enrollee Hold Harmless clause to allow the "collection" of these payments, while leaving the rest of the clause unchanged.

Missouri could now claim that "to collect" and "to bill" are the same under a state's right to interpret its own legislation. Therefore, they could argue they had properly separated the four problem payments from their Hold Harmless clause, thus, making the clause defensible within a state's authority to regulate insurance. However, because the actual language of the bar on billing remained unchanged, insurers were free to continue enforcing it under contract law.

There is just one little problem with all this finagling, if you and I are smart enough to see it. If a provider is barred from "billing" a patient under contract law, how can a provider put a value on *coinsurance, deductibles or copayments,* to "collect" such payments under state law? They can't, because the actual amount of all three is determined from the cost off a "bill" that the Enrollee Hold Harmless clause still strictly forbids when an insurer denies coverage.

So, here we have the most important lesson I have ever learned about the law. It doesn't have to make sense. It just has to be what's stated in the law – a primary reason why so many of us tend to view attorneys as less than honest, because of their ever-so-fine parsing of language to achieve something other than what we would view as justice.

I can't tell you how many states have made a change similar to Missouri. I just haven't taken the time to run it all down. However, I do know that the ones I have looked at have all made the change. So, I have to assume that most, if not all, have made it as well. Because, such a change had to have originated from the NAIC – NAIC being the originator of the Enrollee Hold Harmless language, and the organization responsible for ensuring that the states act uniformly in regulating insurance.

Now, I really hope I have more than made the case for the Unholy Alliance between the insurance industry and government, particularly state government. However, there is an additional piece of evidence that can underline just how ready the states are to aid the insurance industry at our expense.

If you ask your state insurance department about the bar on billing that's in the Enrollee Hold Harmless clause, they will quickly explain that it only applies in instances of insurer insolvency. And, while it's a statement they have every "LEGAL" right to make, it's one that they have zero ethical right to make. Because, in making it, a state is deliberately misleading you and me for the benefit of the insurance industry. It literally can't be anything else. Because the state knows exactly how the American Healthcare System is using the bar. So, it's one meaning for us, and a completely different meaning for the insurance industry.

In fact, it's really nothing more than the old watch my right hand while my left hand steals your wallet. But, in this case, it's our government that's at the heart of the steeling. - - - If that doesn't qualify as an Unholy Alliance, I just can't imagine how far a state has to go to create one.

There is a quote at the front of the book that says it all. *"If you don't think healthcare is about power, you haven't been paying attention."* Well, how do you think "power" is achieved if not through state and federal government?

Summing Up What They "Hide"

What we are asked to view as health insurance had a simple beginning. Blue Cross and a number of others simply offered "ALL" the healthcare one would need for a modest monthly charge. And, when Congress threw its support behind these plans by passing the HMO Act of 1973, things were still simple. HMOs were the only game in town and rapidly growing in popularity. However, the growth brought excesses, and the excesses created a need for regulatory oversight – State oversight that produced a requirement for the establishment of Provider Agreements with every in-network provider in the country. Furthermore, these were Provider Agreements that had to contain an Enrollee Hold Harmless clause, be individually negotiated with every in-network provider, and then reviewed and approved by the appropriate state department of insurance. It was a huge undertaking involving millions of individual negotiations and Provider Agreements.

Unfortunately, as successful as HMOs were at expanding the nation's access to healthcare, they were equally unsuccessful at stemming the growth of the cost of healthcare. This created a growing chorus of calls for HMOs to do more – to do a better job of addressing both the cost of healthcare and providing the care our doctor prescribes.

This put HMOs in a real box. They had to make changes in their plans, but didn't want to incur the cost of having to revise their existing Provider Agreements. Fortunately for the insurance industry, HMOs had been the only game in town when the Agreements were written, so there wasn't a need to restrict them to HMOs. So, they weren't. The language in the Agreements didn't limit their use to the HMO form of health insurance.

At the time, it had to have been viewed as extremely fortunate because it allowed insurers to change plans without having to create a new or revised Provider Agreement. Insurers could simply shoehorn the new plan in under their existing Provider Agreements.

It had to have seemed so simple and straightforward. After all, the language of the existing Provider Agreements wasn't limited to HMOs, and there were only a few new plans. So, there wasn't much of a problem operating off a single Provider Agreement. Furthermore, the risks at that time were small and <u>no one was looking</u>. But, then again, how could anyone be looking when the Agreements were being deliberately hidden?

It was a situation very much like walking out onto thin ice. Each step appears to confirm the ice is solid. But, the further one gets from shore, the greater the risk if the ice breaks.

That is exactly where the healthcare insurance industry finds itself today. Emboldened by the success of their ever-greater departures from the terms and conditions contained in their Provider Agreements, the insurance industry now creates and revises their plans without ever looking back – plans that no longer marry with the terms and conditions in their Provider Agreements – plans that only survive through misrepresentation and the System's "Big Lie" – and, plans that the states and the federal government have shown a ready willingness to look the other way in order to support the System and the money it creates for the U. S. economy, and dare I say our politicians.

For more than fifty years the rising cost of healthcare has been a constant problem for the country. And, forecasts show the problem only getting worse. In response, Washington and the states have called for greater and greater efficiency and competition from the System. However, what we never hear is just how far insurers have been allowed to depart from the terms of their Provider Agreements to pursue this greater efficiency and competition – a pursuit that has certainly not produced the sought-after lower cost of healthcare. However, it's a pursuit that has created an absolute gold mine for the participants in the System.

"The price of medical care is the single biggest factor behind U. S. healthcare costs," (Blue Cross Blue Shield). U. S. family doctors earned an average $214,370 a year in 2020, almost twice that of other developed nations. The salary of our nurses is roughly $15,000 per year higher than other developed nations. Our cost for prescription drugs was $1,443 per person compared to $749 per person in other developed nations. *"Healthcare costs are growing at least 2 to 3 times the rate of inflation,"* (Dartmouth Institute for Health Policy). *"Per capita spending on healthcare is estimated to be 50 to 200 percent greater than other*

developed countries," (AMA Journal of Ethics). *"Researchers and physicians alike have struggled to identify specific instances in which treatments should be withheld,"* i.e., rationing won't work. And, *"Reducing the use of these services nationwide would make a negligible impact on healthcare spending,"* (both from AMA Journal of Ethics). Furthermore, the U. S. is spending roughly 19 percent of GDP on healthcare, while other developed nations are spending on the order of 10 percent. Now, can you understand why I have called our healthcare system a gold mine?

Please understand that there is nothing in these citing's that isn't well documented and grounded in the most basic math. In short, the issue driving the rising cost of U. S. healthcare are the prices we have to pay for the healthcare we need – prices needed to support the profits demanded by our private health-care system and Wall Street.

You and I have become no more than a pea in the age-old shell game. Shuffled from here to there without ever knowing exactly where we are, while our health and financial wellbeing are routinely sacrificed on the altar of the American Healthcare System. After-all, what the American people pay for their health-care fuels the profits for 20 percent of the U. S. economy. So, can there be any surprise that Washington and our state politicians refuse to address the real issue behind the cost of healthcare? Because, to question the real issue behind the cost of healthcare would be to go after the goose with the golden egg.

So, in the minds of our politicians, let's not disrupt the profitability of the largest and fastest growing segment in the U. S. economy. Let's kick that can down the road. Let's allow the healthcare segment of the economy to pursue ever greater prof-its and stick the public with the bill, all while loudly claiming to have the public's interests first in mind.

In a world where the rising cost of healthcare and our shrinking access to it are so obvious, how is it possible to "NOT" see such the obvious fleecing of the American people? How can something so obvious go unaddressed?

The answer is there for any and all who wish to see. It's in the evermore complex world of healthcare. Healthcare plans that defy explanation, bills based on some 77,000 different billing codes that can't be understood, and a monopoly based provider system that makes the promise of greater competition a complete joke. Now wrap all this up in a world where we get involved only when we are at our weakest and most dependent on the System, and you have your answer. We are being deliberately denied the care and coverage we are owed by Provider Agreements we are not allowed to see and rationing that the American Healthcare System and our politicians vehemently deny. In addition, it's all under a healthcare "plan," that is being deliberately misrepresented as insurance to reinforce our acceptance of the System's "Big Lie."

But Why the "Big Lie"

Say what you want about the healthcare insurance industry, but these are not stupid people. Faced with overwhelming pressure from government and the nation's employers to rein-in the rising cost of healthcare on one hand, and the promise of ever greater profits on the other, the decision to ration healthcare was a given, i.e., the old "No Brainer." And, why not? By rationing healthcare, the healthcare insurance industry was simply serving the needs of the nation, while freeing itself to make more money. It was an absolute win-win for insurers. The only thing missing was the "HOW" – how to get the toxic issue of rationing past the American people.

That "HOW" came in the form of the "Big Lie." Because, by creating the belief that we owe whatever our insurer fails to pay for our healthcare, the in-network provider is assured of getting paid. Our insurer can simply deny coverage, step back, and allow the provider to bill us for whatever our insurance has failed to pay.

This was a huge development in the nation's managed care approach to healthcare, because, it allowed the insurance industry to claim they were simply lowering the rising cost of healthcare as Congress has demanded. While, in point of fact, they were adding to their own bottom line, i.e., adding to their profits. So, while the growth of this power to ration healthcare has been anything but smooth, it has clearly become a monster in today's healthcare system.

No longer are insurers content with simply denying individual charges on a large bill, or refusing to provide the required Pre-Approval for an expensive procedure. The system has progressed to where an insurer can deny payment on an entire bill or form of treatment. And, by adding ever-higher deductibles and co-payments to their plans, even though their Provider Agreements bar any such restrictions on coverage, insurers have been able to cast this growing power to ration our healthcare and coverage as nothing more than a logical step in providing more affordable "insurance." Which leaves you and me in the position of having to pay a growing bill we can't begin to understand, and in a System where everyone wins but us.

However, there's another equally important reason for the promotion of the "Big Lie." By keeping us arguing about coverage, the American Healthcare System avoids having to discuss the denial of care that is absolutely barred by their Provider Agreements. We are, instead, instinctively drawn to arguing for greater coverage, when the real issues are the care we are owed and the appropriateness of any bill we get for receiving that care. Or in simpler words, they owe us the care and have "NO" right to bill us. Period!

As long as you and I can be made to continue viewing our healthcare "plan" as insurance, we will continue fighting the wrong war. We will fight the cost of healthcare, which is completely outside our control. And, we will fight the cost of our supposed health insurance, which is again completely outside our control. What we won't do is fight the rationing of our healthcare that is completely at odds with the terms of the system's Provider Agreements.

As I said earlier, these are smart people. So they are going to hide their rationing and hide it well. And, how better to hide it than to keep us focused on the trauma created by a large and unexpected healthcare bill – a bill that is all too easily enforced through the "Big Lie," and something we only need to experience once in our life to lose more than we can afford to lose.

Lastly, we need to address a question that the book must have raised early on, and this is as good a point in the book as any. - - - Why would a healthcare insurance company or plan want to prevent you or me from paying for our own healthcare? - - - The answer is really quite simple.

If our insurer denies coverage, and we are able to get the care by simply paying for it, we would create a prima facie claim for coverage and reimbursement that would be a slam-dunk case in court.

Doctors can only render "medically necessary" healthcare. And, since our doctor prescribed and rendered the care we received, it can only have been "medically necessary" and care that is specifically <u>covered by our plan</u>. Furthermore, because the insurer's denial of coverage could be shown to be part of a system specifically designed to circumvent the authority of an attending physician, we could be potentially looking at punitive damages designed to end the practice altogether. - - - So, it's just so much more efficient for our insurer or plan to ensure we never get the care that's being prescribed and avoid all that legal liability and mess, i.e., liability that could literally bring down the roof on the entire American Healthcare System and its "<u>uniquely American Gold Rush</u>."

So, keep the American people off balance and confused with changing plans that defy description. Blur our understanding of coverage and our shrinking access to affordable healthcare. And, most important, keep the "Big Lie" alive and well to mask it all.

Chapter IV

*"Healthcare should be
affordable for everyone"*
Ed Pastor

How We Got Here
Some Background

The number of books, reports, papers and articles dedicated to analyzing the various products and plans in our managed-care health insurance is nothing less than mind-blowing – HMO, PPO, POS, MCO, HDHP, HAS, etc. Yet nowhere in all this mountain of material have I ever found a single mention of what makes all these acronyms, products and plans one and the same. In my mind, it can only be seen as an indication of just how successful the healthcare insurance industry has been in hiding their Provider Agreements.

Yes, HMOs are different from PPOs, and PPOs are different from POSs, and so on. But, each of these products or plans is centered on using the same network of approved providers and operating off a single Provider Agreement. One Agreement that allows an insurer to change their coverage and plans however and whenever they choose. One Agreement that effectively makes all the different plans one and the same in form and function.

As a way of proving my point, ask yourself this. If we were to look at all the hospitals in the country, do you really think Blue Cross has a separate Provider Agreement with every hospital for every one of Blue Cross' many and changing plans? No way! Not even close to being possible.

It's pretty much like comparing a bottom line Chevrolet with a top of the line model without understanding that they both have the same mechanical structure. All that is really different between the models is what you are allowed to see, and Chevrolet chooses to promote – bigger, shinier, and with more attractive trim and accessories. However, underneath all the glitz is the very same automobile.

The point is that once you understand that all the various managed-care plans and products have the same underlying Provider Agreement, the world health insurance takes on a whole new light. *"The differences between HMO and PPO have blurred,"* and *"a significant majority of consumers do not know which type of plan they have,"* and *"comparing competing plans can be difficult even for sophisticated consumers"* because "important" information is *"often not available."* These are direct quotes from The Market Structure of the Health Care Industry, Congressional Research Service.

Given that roughly 90 percent of the American public have a managed-care healthcare plan, you and I can be confident we do as well, just as long as we have what we are asked to view as health insurance. However, that's about the only thing we have been told about our health insurance that isn't deliberately misleading or false. So, I am going to argue, that if we could actually take a look under the hood of our insurance, it would have all the credibility of a 1929 Ford painted-up to resemble a 2023 Daytona race car. 1929 being the start of what we know today as health insurance.

A Bill Like "NO" Other

Whether it's a breakfast at McDonalds, the purchase of gardening supplies at Home Depot, or the purchase of a new Ford Mustang, we are sure to get a bill that lists all the individual charges that go into the bill – a list of charges that are totaled to arrive at what we owe, and a list of charges we can review to confirm the accuracy and the appropriateness of the bill. Every bill but one.

The in-network healthcare bill is a clear and bold exception to all the other bills in the country. That's because an in-network healthcare bill, unlike all the other bills we get, is missing the information we need to compute what's actually owed. Worse yet, the coverage that our plan claims can range from a low of something like 50 percent to a high of something on the order of 80 or 90 percent for a single line item is "not" to be found. And, in the case of a large hospital bill, where an insurer has very likely completely denied coverage for some individual charges, the bill is completely silent.

Taken collectively, this missing information makes an in-network healthcare bill impossible to verify and one that can only be accepted on blind faith. Furthermore, it's blind faith that I find hard to believe anyone has for the healthcare insurance industry, particularly when the CFPB has ruled that these bills are *"rife"* with error – or in the author's jargon, a bill like "NO" Other.

Chapter V

....

"Healthcare is a right,
not a privilege"
Edward Kennedy.

The World of Managed-Care
The "Beginning"

In the early 1900s, people literally either lived or died when they were injured or got sick. That's because there was very little healthcare available. In addition, the healthcare that was available was only accessible to a privileged few, and even there it was limited to avoiding disease, performing only the most basic surgery, extensive nursing care, and a great deal of praying for recovery. However, technology was on the move. Lister had discovered the importance of antiseptics. Scientists at Eli Lilly were producing reliable quantities of insulin, and we had a cure for smallpox. We had entered the age of scientific healthcare. Unfortunately, this new age came with a significant increase in the cost of healthcare. Where hospitalization had cost the average American family 7.6 percent of their total medical expenses in 1918, that figure had risen to 13 percent by 1929.

Obviously, one can't mention the year 1929 without addressing the impact the Great Depression had on healthcare in the United States. According to Pulitzer Prize-winning author Paul Starr, *"In just one year after the crash, average hospital receipts per person fell from $236.12 to $59.26."* This precipitous drop in hospital revenue came on top of the AMA's (American Medical Association) 1927 published concern about *"the inability of people to pay the cost of modern scientific medicine."* Consequently, the threat of hospital insolvency created by the 1929 crash, together with the rising cost of healthcare, had many believing that necessary healthcare was getting well beyond the reach of the average American family.

It was the perfect storm. The nation's hospitals were facing insolvency, and the AMA had concluded that *"Even among the highest-income group, insufficient care is the rule."* Furthermore, a story in *The New York Times* declared *"Social Medicine Is Urged in Survey."* The fallout generated by all this concern gave birth to what we now call managed-care health insurance in the form of the Blue Cross Association.

Although there were a number of other isolated examples of this new form of health insurance, the perfect storm created by the Great Depression and the ability of what would become the Blue Cross Association to organize hospitals, provided the launching pad for today's employer-supplied managed-care health insurance. Hospitals desperately needed a guaranteed source of income, and the American public needed a source of affordable health care. The plans of the future Blue Cross Association fulfilled both needs. Hospitals got the guaranteed payments they needed to remain solvent, and enrollees in these early plans got a guarantee of "ALL" the healthcare they would need for a small monthly payment.

By charging each enrollee in the plan a small monthly fee or premium, the plan was able to collect the money needed to pay the operational costs of the hospitals it had chosen to work with. This was the same third-party payment system that the American Healthcare System refers to as managed-care, and you and I are led to believe is our very own health "insurance."

The design is very much like a home builder who subcontracts the construction of a house, and then requires periodic payments to be able to pay the subcontractors as they complete the work on the house.

In truth, I just don't see the home builder doing anything much different from a managed-care insurance company. They both collect money up front and then pay subcontractors to do the actual work. The only meaningful difference that I can see between the two is that the builder calls himself a "builder," and the managed-care plan insists on being called an "insurance" company. But, I digress.

The success of the early Blue Cross plans forced hospitals to organize into networks of hospitals in an effort to limit what they saw as inter-hospital competition. These networks then merged into a single organization known as the American Hospital Association, which adopted the name *Blue Cross Association* in 1939.

And, because these early plans were designed by hospitals to benefit hospitals, they covered all hospital expenses right down to the most trivial and inexpensive element of care — all "necessary and appropriate" care. After all, hospitals weren't concerned about controlling the cost of healthcare. They were focused on getting paid. It's a model for coverage that the market would never allow the healthcare insurance industry to change.

By the mid-1930s, the success of prepaid hospital plans, along with the nation's drift toward national health insurance, had physicians worried. They were particularly worried that hospitals would expand their plans into physician services. Physicians reacted by forming their own third-party prepaid plans, which became the Blue Shield Association. These plans then merged with Blue Cross to form the Blue Cross Blue Shield Association we know today as simply Blue Cross.

While it's easy to view the history of Blue Cross and Blue Shield as a fight for control of the developing U. S. healthcare market, it was anything but that. It was simply a fight for control of their respective markets. Because Blue Cross was controlled by hospitals, its focus was on getting their participating hospitals appropriately paid for the services they provided. And, because Blue Shield was controlled by doctors, it was focused on getting their doctors appropriately paid.

Others in the private sector were quick to recognize the opportunity being created by the success of the Blue Cross Blue Shield plans. However, they were effectively forced to adopt the same business model. The small monthly payment to a third party for "ALL" the healthcare one might need was simply too popular for anything else to be competitive.

In 1939 just six percent of the U. S. population had any kind of private health insurance covering hospitalization. However, by 1941 that number had risen to 12.4 percent, with 51 percent covered by a Blue Cross Blue Shield plan. And, by 1945 the number had risen to 23 percent of the entire U. S. population, with 59 percent covered by a Blue Cross Blue Shield plan.

The Rise of the "HMO"

Managed-care plans continued to grow throughout the 1950s and 1960s as groups across the country sought to provide affordable healthcare for their workers or membership. However, the growth lacked the spark needed to make it the national phenomenon it is today. That spark came in 1971 when President Nixon announced a national healthcare strategy built on the development of Health Maintenance Organizations, or HMOs as they are more commonly known. In truth, Nixon's new strategy was simply a new name and acronym for the plans the Blue Cross Blue Shield Association had been supplying since 1929, i.e., all the care you need for a small monthly payment.

However, both cost containment and coverage for the uninsured had become serious political issues for the Nixon Administration. Given that Congress had discouraged individuals from purchasing their own health insurance by: 1.) Making the premiums employers paid for health insurance tax deductible in 1942, and 2.) Eliminating the need for private insurance after age 65 by passing Medicare in 1965, the plans offered by the Blue Cross Blue Shield Association offered a readily available private sector solution for the problems the Nixon Administration was facing. Companies had shown themselves willing to supply health insurance as a tax-exempt employee benefit, and Medicare eliminated the cost of insuring an individual once an employee reached retirement age. Furthermore, it was widely believed that the size and market power of these managed-care plans, or HMOs as President Nixon had chosen to call them, could reign-in the rising cost of healthcare by negotiating lower prices from their in-network providers.

But, there was another driving force that caused Nixon to go all-in on the nation's support for the HMO. It was, that by doing so, he could sidestep the growing calls for national health insurance, and put the country squarely on the path to a private-sector solution for the American Healthcare System.

The overall result was that Nixon put the full weight of the federal government behind the growth of employer-supplied HMOs and gave them the primary responsibility for controlling the rising cost of healthcare. Nixon's stated goal was to go from thirty HMOs in 1970, to 1,700 by 1976, with forty million enrollees and ninety percent of the population enrolled by 1980. In essence, the race to today's 4-trillion dollar healthcare market was off and running.

In 1973 Congress codified President Nixon's HMOs by passing the HMO Act of that same year, which established Nixon's HMO strategy as the law of the land. The Act not only provided funding for developing HMOs, but required employers with twenty-five or more employees to provide an HMO for their employees.

Congress gave these developing HMO plans an additional boost in 1979 by passing the Employee Retirement Income Security Act (ERISA), which essentially eliminated HMO liability for any denial of coverage or care. Sound familiar?

The Role of HMOs in "Controlling" Costs

By the time Congress passed the HMO Act of 1973, the country had experienced forty years of health insurance that provided "ALL" the healthcare a patient needed – forty years devoid of any effort to ration care or curb the cost of healthcare – forty years of simply honoring the role of the attending physician to prescribe the care an individual needed – forty years of paying for "ALL" the healthcare an insured individual's doctor said was needed – and forty years of simply adjusting premiums to cover the cost of the care provided. The HMO Act of 1973 changed everything.

By passing the HMO Act, Congress not only made HMOs the primary tool for curbing the cost of health care, but committed the federal government to supporting the growth of employer-supplied managed-care health insurance, i.e., the HMO.

Not coincidently, insurers immediately began converting to for-profit businesses. Prior to this, the American Healthcare System was comprised largely of nonprofit service organizations. However, the opportunity for almost unlimited growth and profits created by rise of HMOs dramatically changed the game. Healthcare in the United States was forever changed to the profit-driven business model that dominates Wall Street and the investment community to this very day. As a result, the forty-year model of paying for "ALL" the care an enrollee's doctor prescribed was placed in direct conflict with the cost cutting expectations of Congress and the profit demanded by Wall Street. It was a conflict that would only grow as the nation's nonprofit, service-oriented, health care system converted to a market-based, for-profit, business model.

Yes, these new for-profit managed-care insurance companies could pursue greater cost control, as well as greater profitability, by negotiating lower prices from their in-network providers as Congress had envisioned. But, insurers had been exercising that cost-cutting power for forty years and the problems of cost-control and affordability were only getting worse. In short, there was clearly a law of diminishing returns at work and a need for something more if insurers were to deliver the financial performance expected by Congress and demanded by Wall Street. That something could be only the ability to control the healthcare we would be allowed to receive, or at a minimum, the ability to ration the more expensive forms of healthcare that a doctor might prescribe. In essence, the new for-profit managed-care insurance companies saw themselves having to manage the care that the enrollees in their plans could receive.

It should go without saying that there is no better way for an insurance company, or any company for that matter, to cut costs than to simply stop paying for things. And, that is exactly what HMOs began doing to ration healthcare. Doctors were openly accused of overprescribing and the determination of "necessary and appropriate" healthcare was viewed as subjective at best. Furthermore, the law only required insurers to deliver a reasonable "average" standard of care to escape liability for overruling a doctor in deciding "necessary" healthcare." Therefore, HMOs were essentially free to continue promoting their forty-year promise of "ALL" the care an enrollee might need, but make their own determination of just what that care would be.

And, that's exactly what they did. They kept the established promise of "ALL" the care you and I would need, but made the denial of coverage and payment (the rationing of healthcare) their primary tool for delivering the financial performance demanded by Congress and Wall Street – a practice that grew rapidly *"when big for-profit insurers began to take over,"* as stated in the book *Deadly Spin* by whistleblower Wendell Potter.

Mr. Potter's book provides numerous examples of just how far the managed-care healthcare insurance industry has been willing to go to ration healthcare and enhance their financial performance. His <u>*firsthand*</u> account of sixteen-year-old Nataline Sarkisyn can bring tears to the eyes of even the strongest among us.

Nataline suffered from leukemia, but had essentially beaten the disease. However, the treatments she had received to save her life had damaged her liver, and without a transplant, she would not survive. Doctor after doctor not only prescribed a liver transplant as necessary and appropriate healthcare for Nataline, but repeatedly pleaded with CIGNA (her insurer) to agree to cover the cost of the operation. CIGNA refused, substituting their own determination of "necessary and appropriate" care for the findings of Nataline's doctors. Quoting from Mr. Potter's book, *"The company stood by its decision"* and *"The surgery would not meet CIGNA's definition of medical necessity."*

The end result was that Nataline died while CIGNA worked feverishly to protect its image by steadfastly maintaining that the transplant was *"outside the scope of CIGNA's coverage"* (again a direct quote from Wendell Potter's book). Mr. Potter further explains that *"If a critically ill patient dies after an insurance company refuses to pay for a doctor-ordered procedure, which often happens, it can never be proved that the patient would have survived the procedure."* That is to say, there was no downside for CIGNA in denying the care Nataline needed and allowing her to die.

Mr. Potter's firsthand account of the decision-making in a

large insurance company should leave little doubt that managed-care health insurance is all about the money rather than the care you and I may need. Not coincidentally, the title of Chapter VII in Mr. Potter's book, *Deadly Spin*, is "It's All About the Money."

A Big "Bump" in the Road

While the 1980s and 1990s were a period of unbelievable growth for HMOs, the period also produced a big bump in the road for the insurance industry. Backed by the full weight of the Federal Government, the growth of HMOs exploded. By 1986, 156 million employees and their dependents were covered by a major managed-care HMO. Unfortunately, explosive growth generally comes with a cost, and it did here as well. By 1989 the overheated healthcare insurance market had created a number of unsettling insurer bankruptcies. The largest being Maxicare Health Plans. Most troubling was that Maxicare was granted protection under the Federal Bankruptcy Code, which threatened the very authority of the states to regulate health insurance. Equally troubling were the widely reported horror stories of HMOs denying (rationing) critically needed healthcare, which was creating a serious HMO backlash in public opinion. Taken together, the two issues not only threatened the authority of the states to regulate health insurance, but threatened the very structure of the private healthcare insurance system Congress had created.

Surprisingly, the states and the insurance industry found themselves on the same page when it came to finding a solution.

The granting of Chapter 11 protection for Maxicare under the Federal Bankruptcy Code marked a significant departure from what had been the prevailing view of the law. Because, the Federal Bankruptcy Code specifically excludes a "domestic insurance company" from receiving such relief. It's an exception in the law aimed at protecting the authority of the states to regulate insurance. And, while later rulings would appear to make the Maxicare decision an exception, the significance of the threat it created for the states can't be overstated. Because, **the reasoning the court used in reaching its decision on Maxicare was inescapable. HMOs and managed-care health plans are**

"NOT" insurance. They are third-party prepaid "providers" of health care services, a point I made earlier in the book. In fact, this position of the court has never been reversed or resolved. Which caused the Norton Institute on Bankruptcy Law to conclude that in the case of HMOs, *"absent an expressed classification under section 109 of the Federal Bankruptcy Code or some federal statute, the classification of an entity should generally follow the law of the state of incorporation, so long as that classification does not frustrate the purpose of the Code."* Legalese mumbo-jumbo for saying managed-care should be ruled insurance if a state says it's insurance, or it may not be insurance if the state fails to call it insurance. And, you and I are supposed to believe healthcare is a fair and aboveboard system?

While the turmoil that erupted around the Maxicare decision could well be described as a turf war, there was a much greater underlying issue. To the credit of the states, their focus was on protecting the rights of the individual enrollees in these bankrupt HMOs, rather than the rights of a bankrupt insurance company or its in-network providers. However, the Federal Bankruptcy Code bars any such preferential treatment for enrollees. In fact, the federal court's ruling in the Maxicare case described the state's efforts to protect enrollees as *"an anathema to the basic tenant of federal bankruptcy law."*

Where state oversight allows a state to quickly shut down a bankrupt insurer and transfer the enrollees to another plan, federal bankruptcy bars any such quick resolution of insurer insolvency. Under federal bankruptcy protection, an insolvent insurer is guaranteed the right to largely ignore the needs of its enrollees for months, if not years, while it develops a restructuring plan and submits it to the court for approval.

In addition, under federal bankruptcy protection, providers can simply turn to the enrollees in the bankrupt plan for payment, which is an anathema to what the states saw as an appropriate solution for a bankrupt insurance company.

Fortunately, the bankrupt HMOs only wanted to be viewed as noninsurance businesses in the specific instance of their insolvency. That's because there are just too many advantages to being an insurance company. For instance, insurance companies are excluded from federal law restricting monopolies – a huge advantage for large insurance companies with their regional monopolies across the country. So, the question of the states' authority to regulate health insurance effectively solved itself with everyone agreeing to simply label these plans as insurance.

As for addressing the growing HMO backlash in the country by reining-in the power of HMOs to ration healthcare, the states and the insurance industry really had to be on the same page. For, while the public was demanding that the states restrict the power of HMOs to deny coverage, the states couldn't strip HMOs of what Congress viewed as their primary tool for controlling the cost of healthcare. The logic was inescapable. Congress had created HMOs to negotiate lower costs and <u>eliminate unnecessary care and treatment</u>, i.e., ration the care we receive – the unanimous opinion of Justice Souter and the U. S. Supreme Court in Pegram v. Herdrich.

Consequently, the only course open to the states and the insurance industry was to find a way that would appear to provide greater control over HMOs, while allowing them to continue rationing healthcare – but, outside the view of the public.

A Solution Set in "Concrete"

The solution the states and the insurance industry needed came in the form of an HMO Model Act drafted by the National Association of Insurance Commissioners' (NAIC) in the early 1990s. This model piece of legislation was adopted state by state across the country to provide a unified approach to the problems HMOs were facing.

The NAIC is the U. S. standard-setting and regulatory support organization governed by the insurance commissioners from the fifty states, the District of Columbia, and the five U. S. territories. Its published mission is to: 1.) Protect the public interest; 2.) Promote competitive markets; 3.) Facilitate fair and equitable treatment of insurance customers; 4.) Promote the reliability, solvency, and financial solidity of insurance institutions; and 5.) Support and improve state regulation of insurance.

So, while the form and function of managed-care health insurance hadn't changed appreciably since its inception in 1929 and passage of the HMO Act of 1973, the changes in state law brought on by the Maxicare scare, and the adoption of the NAIC's Model Act set this form and function in solid concrete. After all, the backlash of the 1990s had proven that it's one thing for insurers to have the power to ration healthcare, and quite another to exercise it under the watchful eye of the public.

The lesson being that, yes the nation needed an insurance industry capable of rationing healthcare in order to rein-in the rising cost of healthcare. HOWEVER, the insurance industry understood that their means of rationing healthcare had to be kept outside the view of the public. For, to do otherwise would have not only made insurers liable for their denials of care, but assured a strong negative reaction from the public.

The states' adoption of the NAIC's Model Act gave both the insurance industry and the states just what they needed. It not only gave insurers the ability to continue rationing healthcare, it allowed them to do it under a fog of misleading definitions and appeal procedures that gave the appearance of protecting the individual enrolled in an HMO. This appearance was then enhanced by the secrecy that the states assigned to the Provider Agreements that were required by their adoption of the Act.

Heralded as a way to protect enrollees from insurer insolvency and inappropriate denials of coverage, NAIC's HMO Model Act reinforced the states' authority to regulate health insurance, while guaranteeing insurers the **authority to continue rationing healthcare by denying doctors, hospitals, and other in-network providers of healthcare "any" compensation what-so-ever unless they accept an insurer's decision on the healthcare an insured individual should receive.** Or, more simply put, no one gets paid unless the insurer's choice of healthcare is accepted.

In other words, by creating a host of new requirements for HMOs, the states conveyed the impression that they were protecting enrollees, i.e., protecting you and me. However, outside the view of the public, they guaranteed insurers the right to continue rationing healthcare through the creation of secret Provider Agreements with essentially every doctor, hospital and provider of healthcare services in the country. Which, effectively set the form and function of the "private" U. S. healthcare insurance system and the American Healthcare System in solid "concrete." Therefore, as long as you and I get our health insurance from our employer or purchase it directly from a healthcare insurance company, it's essentially certain that we have a managed-care plan that operates through a network of providers with signed Provider Agreements that do not distinguish between HMO, PPO, HDHP or however your insurer has chosen to label a plan.

There is an experience that I had as a general manager for one of DuPont's smaller businesses that can serve as an example of where the insurance industry finds itself with its one size fits all Provider Agreements.

As head of one of DuPont's many businesses, I had a need to establish contracts for our overseas operations. It was a need that came up rather regularly, so I routinely signed these contracts after a review by DuPont's legal department. However, after one particular contract was signed, a larger DuPont businesses objected vigorously and said they would be ignoring the provisions of the contract I had signed. However, DuPont Legal was quick to point out that there was only one DuPont Company, and once I had signed as DuPont, there was no going back and ignoring the provisions of the contract by another DuPont business unit. There was just one DuPont, and one signed and binding contract for the entire DuPont Company.

The healthcare insurance industry finds itself in much the same position as that large DuPont business unit. Because they wrote just one universal HMO Provider Agreement – a contract that: 1.) Is simply in their Corporate Name (as we did at DuPont), 2.) Only identifies the insured as "enrollees," or something equally nonspecific, 3.) Requires providers to provide all necessary healthcare regardless of whether the insurer agrees to cover the cost, 4.) Bars the provider from billing either the insurer or the enrollee when coverage is denied, and 5.) Bars any and all disclosure of the Agreement. This then yielded two things. One, the Provider Agreements apply to every plan an insurer markets regardless of what an insurer chooses to call a particular plan, and two, insurers can't distinguish between enrollees in their different plans because their Provider Agreements provide no such separation or distinction.

Stating the above as simply as I can, the insurance industry's Provider Agreements do "NOT" allow insurers to assign different provisions for their different plans or enrollees. They are all "ONE."

However, there is one very significant benefit that the insurance industry's one-size fits all Provider Agreements has allowed insurers to take to the bank. It's the ability to change plans without ever having to change a Provider Agreement. This is a huge benefit because of the cost and complexity of changing so many Agreements so often, while allowing the insurance industry to steadily ratchet-up their rationing to pass more and more of the cost of healthcare to you and me. In addition, this one-size fits all design is a huge benefit to the States, because it avoids having to review and approve millions of Provider Agreements on a yearly basis.

One Agreement that is locked away never to be seen by you, me or the American people. And, one Agreement that only survives because the States and Congress have chosen to look the other way.

Chapter VI

*"Whenever a doctor
cannot do good, he
must be kept from
doing harm:"*
Hippocrates

Why "Me" & the Book
The "Death" of Sandy

My introduction to the rationing hidden in the American Healthcare System and the "Big Lie" came with a heavy price – the death of my first wife, Sandra Sargisson Lobb, or simply Sandy, as we knew her. A softly spoken woman who had been raised in the absence of love and had struggled to find her place in life. It was a struggle that involved periodic disappearances into alcoholism, but one that never blurred her view of the responsibility she owed to our three children, family and friends. In fact, Sandy was like far too many in life who need help, and deserve far better than the American Healthcare System is prepared to allow.

I've told this story so many times I won't dwell on it here. However, what I will do is simply describe what happened to Sandy as an example of just how far the American Healthcare System and the healthcare insurance industry are willing to go to ration healthcare, and provide a why for me and the book.

We were a family like so many others that simply assumed the health insurance we got from our employer would be there when we needed it. We also thought that we could purchase any healthcare our insurance failed to cover. Furthermore, we never doubted for even one moment the trust and confidence we placed in our family doctor.

All these blind-faith assumptions changed overnight when our health insurance denied Sandy the hospital care her doctor insisted she needed to save her life. Care and coverage that was guaranteed by Pennsylvania Law. And, care and coverage that we thought were absolutely guaranteed by our health insurance. However, that was only the beginning of my introduction to the real world of health insurance and the plan the American Healthcare System deliberately hides.

The real zinger came when the hospital told me that the contract they had with our insurer (their Provider Agreement) prevented them from allowing me to pay for the care Sandy needed. In other words, our insurer was not only refusing to cover the care Sandy needed, they were contractually barring the hospital from allowing me to pay for it. An admission that only came after a lengthy session where I browbeat the manager of the hospital unmercifully.

The bottom line is that Sandy died while I sputtered and fumed over how an insurance company could stop me from paying for the lifesaving care Sandy needed.

What followed were 8 long years of suing our insurance company through 3 courts in an effort to get justice for Sandy. Not because we had been denied coverage for the care Sandy needed, but because I had been denied the right to pay for it outside of any participation by our insurance company.

Eight long years needed to educate me on just how far the American Healthcare System is willing to go to protect the rationing in the System and "Big Lie." Because, what I only came to understand far too late, was that I wasn't arguing for my right to pay for Sandy's lifesaving care. I was arguing to disclose the hidden rationing in the American Healthcare System and the inherent fraud in the System's "Big Lie." It was a fight that no one remotely connected to the system was going to let me win. So, I sputtered and fumed for 8 long years through three separate courts as the System closed ranks to eventually shut me down.

What made the situation even worse was that everyone I spoke to in the healthcare system and government lied about what was happening. I had clearly been denied the right to pay for Sandy's care. Yet, everyone I went to insisted no such refusal was even possible.

Acting as my own attorney and hard-headed by birth, I drove the case through 3 separate courts as our insurance company fought tooth and nail to keep their Provider Agreement secret and outside the proceedings. The State of Pennsylvania even entered the proceedings in support of our insurer's insistence that their Provider Agreement be kept secret. In fact, the healthcare community closed ranks to such a degree that there came a point where I couldn't even prove how Sandy had died. Records just magically disappeared.

Our insurance company didn't want me to win because it would undercut their power to ration healthcare as well as set a precedent for future cases. The state of Pennsylvania didn't want me to win because they supported the system that allowed the rationing of healthcare. The Federal Government didn't want me to win because the case had the potential to disrupt the entire healthcare system. And, of course, the hospital didn't want me to win because it could lead to all kinds of liability.

What really hurt was when our doctor started backing away as she realized the threat my suite was creating for her practice and her entire way of life. She, along with the other doctors and nurses familiar with the case, began looking at me with a *"What can I do? My career is on the line."*

Most disheartening was the long list of people and organizations that claimed to be advocates for healthcare reform, but wanted no part of disclosing the insurance industry's Provider Agreements, the rationing they foster, or the System's "Big Lie." These people and organizations were so deep into the business of raising money from the System, that they wanted no part of anything that might interrupt the flow of money they were receiving – a reality that only dawned on me after my expressions of outrage over what had happened to Sandy were swept aside like puffs of smoke on a windy day.

Organizations and individuals like Consumer Watchdog, the American Medical Association, Cato Institute, The Heritage Foundation, Americans for Democratic Action, U. S. Representative Joe Pitts, chair of the House Subcommittee on Health, U. S. Senator Robert Casey, AARP, The Institute for Justice, and the ACLU all listened and then simply went away. Yet not one of these organizations or people ever offered a single point of disagreement on a fact or point of law that I described in my book The Great Health Care Fraud. To quote a leading constitutional attorney for one of these groups, **"You are not hearing me. I'm not saying I disagree with you. I'm saying we just don't want to deal with it."**

I won't bore you with the rest of my personal story because it would contribute little to the book. I will add only that my years of litigation forced the opposing attorneys to, bit by bit, surrender the details of the insurer's Provider Agreements and the American Healthcare System's "Big Lie." Clearly this wasn't a win in the eyes of the law and it certainly wasn't the win I wanted for Sandy. However, it was a very big win for me and my family in that we will never again face the rationing that took the life of Sandy, and, we will never again be held hostage to a fraudulent healthcare bill, a denial of care, or the American Healthcare System's "Big Lie."

PART TWO
---The How & Why of the Fraud

Chapter VII

....

*"Take care of the patient and
everything else will follow"*
Samuel Johnson, MD

Pushing "Back"
Laying the "Groundwork"

While it's very likely that the rationing scheme contained in the insurance industry's Provider Agreements could never survive a Constitutional test, it should "NOT" be viewed as a reason for you or me to attack an insurance company through the courts. Furthermore, nothing in the book should be viewed as encouraging any such assault on the American Healthcare System. Or, more simply put, **"Suing" a healthcare insurance company or plan for failing to provide the care, coverage and billing we are owed is a fool's errand!**

When my wife Sandy died because I was denied the right to pay for her healthcare, I sued our insurance company. And, through all the litigation that followed, I never once got the chance to argue the facts in the case to a jury. All I got was motion after motion designed to delay, obfuscate and keep the case as far away from a jury as possible.

The end result was that a federal judge, ruling solely off the insurer's petition to dismiss the case, found that the insurer's

Provider Agreement *"unambiguously allowed payment"* for the care Sandy needed and *"presented no such restricted access to healthcare."* It was a ruling that: 1.) Completely ignored the issue I had put before the court, and 2.) Forever blocked my ability to put the facts in Sandy's death to a jury.

Now, I really hope you can understand the difference between a restriction on PAYING and a restriction on BILLING, because the federal judge clearly didn't. Or, far more likely, he refused to acknowledge the difference so he could dismiss the case for the benefit of the American Healthcare System. He simply equated the two as one and put an end to my case. Never mind that there was absolutely "NO" way I could have paid for Sandy's care if the hospital couldn't bill me for the care she received.

The point I am trying to make is that nothing in the book should be interpreted as encouraging you to sue a healthcare insurance company or plan for failing to provide the care, coverage and billing we are owed.

What the book does do is provide an easy to follow roadmap for pushing back against the American Healthcare System to get the care, coverage and billing we are owed without suing anyone or asking a court to interpret a Provider Agreement that the insurance industry will fight tooth and nail to keep hidden. Most importantly, it's a roadmap specifically aimed at avoiding the *"doom loop"* that the head of CFPB describes as *"all too common for patients and their families"* subjected to the American healthcare billing system. Furthermore, it's a roadmap centered on only having to ask a few simple questions to get a bill stopped dead in its tracks. Thus, lifting an in-network healthcare bill out of the doublespeak and outright fraud in the <u>healthcare billing</u> *"doom loop"* and dropping it instead in the well-settled world of <u>general bill collection</u> **where a healthcare provider or bill collector can be put in the unenviable position of having to explain a bill (<u>which they cannot do</u>) or cancel the debt.**

Let me repeat this point because it's so very important. You and I do **"NOT"** want to take on the "Big Lie," the hidden rationing or the fraudulent billing in the American Healthcare System. We want to stay as far away from presenting that kind of threat to the System as possible. Instead, **we want to push back by simply lifting our unpaid in-network healthcare bill out of the well protected morass of HEALTHCARE billing and put it in the well-settled world of GENERAL bill collection**.

In so doing, we can separate our bill from the protected world of healthcare rationing and subject it solely to the well-settled law governing all bill collection.

When I pursued justice for Sandy through the court, I made the very mistake I am warning against. I attacked the System. I just couldn't bring myself to believe anyone would support a system that was designed to deny me the right to pay for Sandy's care. I completely missed the fact that my suit was attacking the very core of the American Healthcare System Congress created to control the cost of healthcare.

A Far "BETTER" Way

Some months ago my wife and I had back to back appointments with a dermatologist we had been seeing every 6 months for some years. The bill for each of these visits had always been around $40 after insurance. This time, the bill for my wife was once again roughly the same $40. However, mine jumped to $500. We promptly paid my wife's bill, but I wrote back questioning the amount of my bill and asking a few simple questions.

What followed were 2 more copies of the same $500 bill, but without a response to my request for an explanation of the bill. On receiving each of these repeat billings, I wrote back and once again requested an explanation of the bill.

The next thing I got was a fourth copy of the bill, but this time it was from a collection agency informing me they had purchased the bill and would be pursuing collection. Where in, I immediately wrote back informing them that I was exerting my right under the Fair Debt Collection Practices Act to: 1.) Dispute the accuracy of the bill, and 2.) Request a detailed explanation of the bill. I also included a copy of my earlier unanswered letter requesting an explanation of the bill.

"VERY" shortly after that, I got a fifth bill. However, it was once again from the dermatologist and showed a Balance Due of only $40. Which we promptly paid. I then got written confirmation from both the doctor and the collection agency that the bill had been settled.

Rather than attacking the "Big Lie" or arguing my rights under a Provider Agreement that the dermatologist can't discuss, the collection agency has never seen, and the courts don't want any part in resolving, I had simply asked for the understandable explanation of my bill that the law governing all bill collection affords me.

Case won and done. And, won solely by using the law applicable to all "GENERAL" bill collection, while avoiding any threat to the hidden workings of the American Healthcare System. It's the **"silver lining"** in healthcare billing. Because, the bills we receive, as a general rule can't be defended, as long as we ask a few simple questions that we are entitled to ask under the FDCP and the recommendations of the CFPB.

You Are "Literally" On Your Own

I recently took my wife to a specialist for a minor medical procedure and the first thing she was asked to do was to sign an ABN (Advance Beneficiary Notice of Non-coverage). It's a formal contract where you agree to pay whatever Medicare fails to pay, while acknowledging that there is a good chance that the care you are getting might not be covered. The woman at the desk insisted it was just a formality. This was in spite of the fact that my wife and I have three separate health insurance plans.

Serving as my wife's advocate, I pointed out that their use of the ABN was completely inappropriate. The woman then quickly retrieved the form with a very ready "oh, you don't have to sign it."

On our way out of the office after seeing the doctor, we had to stop back to see the same woman who had asked my wife to sign the ABN. I again mentioned the inappropriateness of asking my wife to sign an ABN. And, to support my point, I showed her the cover for the book that I just happened to have with me. She read it, looked up and said *"I am really not allowed to say anything."* I replied, *"I understand."* She then looked back up with this ever-so-big smile on her face and gave me the biggest up and down nod of her head for a yes to the "Big Lie."

Shortly before our above visit to the doctor, my wife and I attended a wedding with a magnificent outdoor reception. The man next to me in the line for the open bar happened to mention that he managed the local hospital. So, I found myself having to ask him about the insurance industry's ability to deny payment whenever they choose. To which he readily agreed and then went on at some length to explain just how difficult these denials of coverage and payment made his life. I then asked him for a business card. He said yes, but that he would have to get one from his coat. And, so began an evening of hide and seek. I knew he was never going to give me his name and card, but I wasn't going to let him skate on his promise to get back to me.

I bumped into the gentleman three more times over the course of the evening and each time he couldn't separate himself fast enough while promising to get right back to me with his business card – just another case of *"I am really not allowed to say anything."*

Then there is a very recent example where my wife and I had a quick dinner at the bar of our local golf club. Sitting next to me was an attorney doing the same thing after finishing a round of golf. I had the book laying on the bar which drew us into a discussion on health insurance. The attorney was jovial, and certainly dismissive, in what he clearly saw as an opportunity to ridicule me and the book. However, what I can only describe as his absolute shock at discovering I had read the insurance industry's Provider Agreements and was completely familiar with their meaning under contract law. It was a realization that only dawned on him after his dismissive questions had failed – questions clearly intended to show how little I knew about the Insurance Industry's Provider Agreements and the American Healthcare System.

It was also a realization that had him up and on his way without ever disclosing his name or position in the System. I can't even say whether he finished his dinner. What I can say is that it wasn't an easy or comfortable departure as he is the only individual I have ever met who had a lawyer's understanding of the insurance industry's Provider Agreements. Believe me, I did everything I could to get his name and contact information before he left without so much as sharing his first name.

I've cited these three examples to make a simple point. The very people you and I would think we could look to for help with a healthcare bill, or to understand the American Healthcare System, have been pulled so far in under the "Big Lie" that they can't afford to be honest with us. Not that the woman at the counter wanted any part of misleading my wife or me, and certainly not that the man I met at the wedding reception, or the attorney I met over dinner at the local golf club, were being intentionally dishonest. However, just as the woman at the doctor's office had so aptly said, *"I am not ALLOWED to say anything."* The operative word being ALLOWED, because the American Healthcare System is ready, willing and able to hurt anyone who would dare step out of line to tell truth about the care and coverage we are owed from our health insurance, or the rationing inherent the System's "Big Lie."

Fortunately, you and I are not a part of the American Healthcare System. We can't be fired or have our careers destroyed. However, the flip side of being safely outside the System is that we can't count on the people in the System for help. In fact, we can't even count on the attorneys and advocates that claim to be willing to take on the System, because they won't understand the details of the System's Provider Agreements and have a financial incentive to keep the system functioning as it is.

Yes, you can readily find an attorney or financial advocate to represent you in settling a healthcare bill. Unfortunately, these are not likely to be people willing to rock the boat or risk having to face the wrath of the American Healthcare System. After all, they earn their living working in the System, so they are likely to have little interest in doing anything that could be seen as attempting to disclose the fraud and rationing in the System, along with its "Big Lie." Furthermore, the cost of litigating any such disclosure would be well beyond any attorney's financial well-being.

The bottom line is that as long as you are willing to accept a discount on a bill, or pay it over some period of time, there is a whole industry of people and companies out there willing to assist you for a fee. But, if like me, you really want to pay no more than you actually owe, that's an entirely different matter. Because, **"We are going to have to fend for ourselves!"**

The Significance of Being "In-Network"

When the protection we expect from law and order vanishes, we often refer to it as the Wild-Wild West. That's exactly how we need to view getting healthcare out of network. Because, once we step outside the billing protections offered by a Provider Agreement, we are literally in the Wild-Wild West of healthcare billing. A world where the average cost for a three day stay in a hospital is $30,000, and the cost for treating cancer can easily run into hundreds of thousands of dollars. So, if that is where you are, please stop right here and hire someone with experience in negotiating an out-of-network healthcare bill.

In a recent meeting with the broker my wife and I use to purchase health insurance for the employees in our family business, we got to discussing PPOs versus HMOs. The broker stressing the ability of a PPO to provide some level of coverage for out-of-network bills. I then said *"I just can't believe PPOs should be counted on for out-of-network healthcare."* The broker's response is frozen in my mind because it was so unexpected and explosive. He said *"Oh God no!"*

The point being that once we step outside of network for healthcare, we step beyond the protections of a Provider Agreement and into a world where our broker's warning of *"Oh God no"* needs to be seen in flashing red lights. Because, we are entering a world where you and I don't have a chance of understanding the 77,000 billing codes used to generate a healthcare bill, and price is essentially a buyer beware issue.

Yes, our health insurance is rank with fraud and both the insurer and their in-network providers are aligned to pick our pocket. But, their hidden Provider Agreements can provide us with a readily available escape from an unreasonable in-network healthcare bill – an escape that simply isn't available for an out-of-network bill.

The American Healthcare System is counting on you and me to allow our healthcare bill to be seen as just another unpaid debt. To have it thrown-in with all the other unpaid bills in the country and treated no differently from an unpaid credit card bill. However, by staying in-network and then demanding the rights guaranteed by the FDCPA and recommended by the CFPB, we can put a whole new spin on the collection of a healthcare bill. However, we first need to get our care, in-network!

Establishing Your "Goal"

The February 2023 edition of Time Magazine carried an article on what it called our "lousy" healthcare system. One of the complaints it mention was the failure of all the calls, letters and efforts requesting help from an insurance company to get any meaningful help with an onerous healthcare bill. That's because it takes a good deal more than a bunch of letters and phone calls to an insurance company to resolve a healthcare billing problem. After all, the problem rests with the provider that sent the bill. Furthermore, the CFPB has cited the healthcare billing system for its *"structural dysfunction and inaccuracy."* So, why be surprised when our insurer fails to act on a bill that isn't theirs in a system that is structurally dysfunctional?

We need to remember that when we look for help with a healthcare bill, we will be just one person in a sea of people arguing for greater coverage and a smaller bill. Something like one out of every four American families is struggling with an unpaid healthcare bill. So, everyone you and I can reach with our letters and phone calls will have heard our story many times over. And, while whoever we contact may appear understanding and even promise to help, you can bet they are working off a script designed to provide an illusion of help while ensuring the window for disputing a bill closes quietly and unnoticed.

Of course, if all you really want is a reduction in a bill, the quickest way to get that is to simply call whoever sent the bill and offer to pay it in exchange for a discount.

However, if your goal is to pay no more than you actually owe, the book is aimed at helping you to do just that. Consequently, the book begins from the premise that all in-network healthcare bills are grounded in fraud and "**UNENFORCEABLE**." Therefore, the book argues your goal should always be the complete cancelation of these unenforceable in-network healthcare bills on the **justification that you are simply pursuing the care and coverage you are "OWED."** Or, stating it in reverse, you should never have to pay more than a provider can legally support under the provisions of the FDCPA and the CFPB.

And, for those who would argue that the book is promoting a means for skipping-out on a healthcare bill by parsing some remote contract language, please consider this: The book is doing nothing more than providing a means of questioning the accuracy of a healthcare bill as the CFPB has advised us to do, and the FDCPA gives every right to do. Nothing More!

Intentional "Fraud" from the Start

To support a charge of fraud under U. S. law, one needs to be able to prove "intent." In other words, one has to be able to show that the one committing the fraud was aware of the misrepresentation and did it to profit at the others expense. So, when I call the "Big Lie" a fraud, I am absolutely certain your healthcare provider and the American Healthcare System will argue they are only using the *"you owe whatever your insurance fails to pay,"* and what I have labeled the "Big Lie," as an expedient means of addressing the wide range of patients they have to bill. Sounds reasonable, right! But, wait a minute. Let's drill down and see just how reasonable the claim is.

The overwhelming majority of people in the United States have some form of health insurance, and whether it's from the government, an employer, or bought privately, the plans all bar billing an insured enrollee when their plan fails to pay for the care they need and receive. The only exceptions are for experimental care, elective cosmetic procedures or care the government specifically excludes for Medicare and Medicaid. So exactly who is the American Healthcare System addressing with their message of "**You assume the financial responsibility of paying for all services not covered by your insurance**"?

So, please, someone tell me who the American Healthcare System is addressing with their *"you owe whatever our insurer fails to pay?"* Roughly 90 percent of Americans have health insurance and only 7 percent get healthcare out-of-network. Which can only leave a miniscule number of patients that qualify for the statement. A miniscule number that shrinks when you re-move the uninsured, for which the *"you owe whatever our insurer fails to pay"* makes no sense at all.

The inescapable conclusion is that the American Healthcare System can only be aiming their *"you owe whatever our insurer fails to pay"* at the vast majority of Americans for which it does not apply and only serves to simplify the recouping of the monies that providers stand to lose when an insurer denies coverage in order to ration healthcare.

Now, I'm not an attorney, and I need to admit that I have often been criticized for using the word "fraud" to describe the "Big Lie." However, I have never shrunk from calling it what it is, and I am not about to do so here. Because, if there has ever been a case of deliberate misrepresentation for financial gain, it's the American Healthcare System's "Big Lie."

The question then becomes, given the book's admonition on suing, how can we use the fraud in the "Big Lie" to push back against a healthcare bill? - - - We put the provider or bill collector in the position <u>of having to either defend the fraud in public, or "quietly" abandon the bill and walk away</u>. In essence, we take the provider or bill collector to a place where they dare not go and cannot go - - - while doing nothing more than asking a few simple questions that the law both affords us and recommends that we ask.

The "Fair Debt Collection Practices Act"

The Fair Debt Collection Practices Act (FDCPA) was passed by Congress back in 1978 for the specific purpose of reining-in the excesses in debt collection that were plaguing the nation. I think it's fair to say that those same excesses exist today in the billing practices of the American Healthcare System. In fact, Bulletin 2022-01: Medical Debt Collection and Consumer Reporting Requirements in Connection With the No Surprises Act published by the U. S. Consumer Financial Protection Bureau (CFPB) makes this very point as well as identifying these excesses as a primary cause of family bankruptcy in the United States. Of particular interest to you and me is that the FDCPA: 1.) Prohibits the use of false, deceptive or misleading representation to collect a bill, 2.)

Requires proof of the validity and appropriateness of a bill when it's requested in writing within 30-days of receiving a bill, and 3.) Prohibits ANY and ALL collection efforts until the requested information is provided.

However, like any federal law, the Act is long and complex in its legalese, and the above description only highlights the main points of the Act. So, please don't start spouting it like it's a cure-all for resolving all unpaid healthcare bills. However, what it clearly is, is a simple way of putting a provider or bill collector in the awkward position of having to "prove" a bill is valid or having to abandon it. Or, as my attorney friend has so aptly put it, making whoever is pursuing payment face the fact that *"it's cheaper to eat it!"*

At first glance, having to prove the accuracy and appropriateness of a bill may seem a trivial matter. However, in the case of an in-network healthcare bill, I can assure you it is anything but. For, while we may not be able to win a court fight over whether an in-network provider has the right to bill us when coverage is denied, we can readily put the provider or collection agency in the unenviable position of having to provide information they either CAN'T afford to disclose, or CAN'T even access.

For, while the FDCPA may not state specifically what information a provider or bill collector has to provide in order to prove the accuracy of a healthcare bill, the CFPB's bulletin entitled Unlawful Medical Debt issued on January 13, 2022, certainly does! It states that *"Consumer financial protection law prohibits debt collectors from misrepresenting the character, AMOUNT, or legal status of any debt,"* and, that there must be a *"reasonable and timely investigation of consumer disputes to verify the ACCURACY"* of a purported healthcare debt. Then on April 11, 2022, the CFPB issued a bulletin entitled Know your Rights and Protections When it Comes to Medical Bills and Collections. Where the CFPB specifically advised: *1.) "Check your bills for accuracy," 2.) Make sure "you received the treatments listed," 3.) "Check the costs for the different procedures and what is and is not covered by insurance," and 4.) "Ask your provider for a plain language explanation for items on medical bills that are unclear to you."* Now add to those requirements the well-accepted description of what a reasonable invoice (bill) should include, namely: **1.) A description of the products and services sold,** and **2.) The quantity and price of each product/service sold**, and we have a ton of very necessary and specific information that the American Healthcare Billing System doesn't want to provide! And, in most cases can't even access let alone disclose.

In short, the System is expecting you and me to flail around protesting the unfairness of a bill or coverage while never PROPERLY DISPUTING it. Thus allowing the bill to sail effortlessly through the collection process to become legally enforceable in court.

To quote the head of CFPB on the Bureau's efforts to protect us from unlawful medical debt, *"We are taking patients out of the middle of the food fight between insurers and providers and ensuring they aren't met with eye-popping, bankruptcy-inducing medical bills."*

The beauty of this quote is that when we add it, along with the actions of the CFPB, to the provisions of the FDCPA, we can have a simple risk-free means of completely reversing the burden of proof on a healthcare bill. Or more simply put, we can completely sidestep the "food fight" the American Healthcare System is counting on to enforce a healthcare bill. Furthermore, we don't have to do anything more than to: 1.) Formally dispute the accuracy and appropriateness of our bill within 30-days (our right under the FDCPA) and, 2.) Require whoever sent the bill to "prove" the accuracy and appropriateness of the bill (in accordance with actions of the CFPB). The fact that the required prof is contractually barred from disclosure or not even assessable isn't our problem. In fact, it's our "get out of jail card" on one of these fraudulent healthcare bills. It's a problem that is entirely of the System's own making.

After all, how can a bill be enforceable, if the one demanding payment can't provide the most basic proof that the bill is accurate?

This is the exact situation I earlier described with the $500 bill I received from my dermatologist. Once faced with the reality that *"it's cheaper to eat it!"* that $500 bill just magically vanished!

Unfortunately, as long as you and I allow the collection of a healthcare bill to be processed as just another unpaid bill, we trap ourselves in the misrepresentation, falsehoods and outright legal bias that comprise the American Healthcare System's "Big Lie." However, by simply applying the requirements of the FDCPA and the CFPB to a healthcare bill we can lift our bill out of the morass of healthcare billing and into the light of day where the risk that we are creating for the System argues that it's simply *"cheaper to eat it."*

This is no small accomplishment. Please believe me! Because, as long as our bill can be viewed as just another unpaid debt, the only issue on the table will be how to force us to pay it. The "Big Lie" of *"we are responsible for whatever our insurer fails to pay"* will be front and center and our bill will have languished for more than 30 days to make it automatically enforceable in court.

To provide some context for just how difficult a position our "properly" disputing the accuracy of a healthcare bill places a provider or bill collector, we only need to consider the following: 1.) The size and complexity of a large healthcare bill, 2.) The 77,000 indecipherable billing codes that the System uses to assign costs, 3.) The healthcare details that HIPPA requires remain private, 4.) Pricing your insurer demands remain hidden, and 5.) The details of coverage for individual charges that your insurer also demands remain hidden.

Even more troubling for your insurer or the provider is having to provide information that is so basic to demonstrating the accuracy of a bill, that a court might simply order the production of the information, i.e. order the production of information that the American Healthcare System is absolutely opposed to disclosing. Like, an itemized bill that seven states and MEDICARE define as a legal right for all patients.

It's the old rock and a hard place. The provider or collection agency wants to pursue payment, but to do so they have to disclose information that is potentially far more damaging to the entire billing system than non-payment of one particular bill. As my lawyer friend said, *"it's cheaper to eat it."*

However, as good as the FDCPA and the CFPB are at shifting the burden of proof away from you and me and onto whoever is pursuing payment of a bill, there is a critical requirement that cannot be overstated. To have the FDCPA apply, **we have to formally "dispute" the bill in writing within 30 days of receiving it**. Yes, I have repeated this point far too often. But, if we miss the 30-day window for the FDCPA, we allow a court to automatically conclude a bill is valid for collection. Our ability to dispute the accuracy of the bill is effectively dead in the eyes of a court. Case closed, issue settled, and we owe whatever the bill says we owe. All that will remain of our efforts to contest a bill will be how and when we have to pay it.

Haven't you ever wondered why providers or collection agencies are so willing to allow a bill to languish for 60 to 90 days? They are allowing the bill to "ripen" for picking.

Quoting directly from the CFPB, *"You have 30 days to dispute a debt or part of a debt"* and, *"Once you dispute the debt, the debt collector can't call or contact you to collect the debt or the disputed part until the debt collector has provided verification of the debt in writing to you."*

And

"There are strong reasons to exercise your right to request validation of a debt."

And

"If you dispute the debt in writing within 30 days - - - the debt collector must stop all collection activity until it provides the required verification" of the debt.

Please understand that the FDCPA is typically viewed as only applying to those in the business of debt collection, or a debt collection agency. However, you are only asking for proof that a bill is accurate from an industry that is notorious for its inaccurate billing. Furthermore, once properly requested in writing, your letter has to be made a permanent part of the billing record, and per the stated position of CFPB, steps have to be taken to demonstrate the "ACCURACY" of the bill. Consequently, for a provider to send a bill to collection without having provided the proof you have requested is a violation of consumer protection law per the CFPB. Furthermore, if the bill goes to collection without you having received the proof you requested, you will only need to send a copy of your request to the collection agency to effectively tie the System in knots. After all, the entire premise of the bill collection process in the American Healthcare System is to allow a bill to languish for more than 30 days so that it becomes legally enforceable purely on its face, i.e., no explanation or justification needed to enforce the bill.

But What If I Miss the 30-Day Window

While the book is focused on disputing a bill within the 30-day window required by the FDCPA, there will be readers who are well beyond this 30-day window. So, what are they supposed to do? How can they dispute an unreasonable healthcare bill?

There are two potential solutions. The first is to simply ignore the 30-day requirement and follow the steps suggested in the book for disputing a bill. After all, the primary threat posed by the FDCPA is "having" to disclose the details of a Provider Agreement in order to proceed with a collection process. That threat still exists in the rulings of the CFPB. So, all that will have been lost by failing to dispute a bill within the 30-day window of the FDCPA is the ability to stop a collection process as a matter of law.

An alternative approach would be to have an attorney petition the court for an extension of the 30-day window based on the misrepresentation and fraud attached to the bill. Namely, that: 1.) Both the insurer and the provider have deliberately hidden the provisions of their Provider Agreement that prohibit the bill, 2.) The CFPB has ruled that these bills are "rife" with error and must be subjected to a rigorous examination capable of demonstrating the accuracy of the bill, and 3.) The provider's representation that the Plaintiff is *financially responsible for whatever the insurer has failed to pay*" is blatantly false and a deliberate misrepresentation for the purpose of denying the Plaintiff his or her "right" to dispute the accuracy and appropriateness of the bill within the 30-day window.

In either case, there would have to be a hearing to decide how to move forward with the collection of a bill. Consequently, the collection agency may choose to just walk away and avoid the hearing, rather than risk having to disclose information it can't access, along with an inability to confirm the accuracy of the bill as required by the CFPB.

While one can never be certain just how a court would rule on either approach, the insurer, the provider and the collection agency will have the very same problem. And, they will have far more to lose than an individual disputing a single bill. In fact, we will have essentially nothing to lose, other than possibly of having to pay the bill. While the parties responsible for a bill will be putting the entire healthcare billing system at risk unless they abandon the bill and any court hearing on the issue.

Chapter VIII

*The interests I have to believe
in a thing is no more proof that
such a thing exists*
                                    Voltaire

How to "Dispute" a Bill
Requesting an "Explanation" of your Bill

The entire billing system of the American Healthcare System is built on "NOT" providing an understandable bill. The intent being to never have to disclose the pricing, discounting and coverage decisions that are used to ration healthcare, as well as provide a basis for a dysfunctional healthcare billing system. After all, how better to deal with all this inherent complexity in healthcare billing than to simply burry the problem under the well-promoted claim that *"we owe whatever our insurance fails to pay."*

Fortunately, the FDCPA and the CFPB can provide us with an excellent way to discredit that claim. In fact, a great example of what the book is proposing can be found in the events of the subprime mortgage crisis in 2008.

Prior to 2008, the nation's banks had sold untold numbers of subprime mortgages. They then bundled them and traded them back and forth to such an extent that they lost the supporting documentation for individual mortgages. Consequently, when the economy collapsed and homeowners began defaulting on these mortgages, the banks were unable to foreclose.

It wasn't a case of whether there was a mortgage or it was unpaid. Those facts were clear to everyone. It was simply that the courts required the supporting documentation for a mortgage in order for a bank to foreclosure on a mortgage, and the banks couldn't provide that documentation. So, the banks couldn't foreclose even after a homeowner had long ago stopped paying on the mortgage and abandoned the property.

Simply put, it wasn't that the homes didn't have a mortgage or that money wasn't owed on the mortgage. It was simply that the banks couldn't produce the documents that the law required to foreclose on a mortgage.

The legal system can provide another example how an issue can be brought to a standstill. In civil law, it's very common for the respondent to a complaint or suit to file what are called preliminary objections. The whole purpose of the filing being not to question the alleged damage or injustice claimed in the suit, but rather to simply dispute the right of the individual (more properly referred to as "standing") to put the matter before the court. Lacking that standing, the case can't go forward and must be summarily dismissed regardless of any actual damage or injustice in the case.

Fortunately for you and me, the American healthcare System can be made to face this same quandary. Namely, if the System can't provide the documentation the law requires to enforce a healthcare bill, then just as in the two examples above, the bill can't move forward, i.e. it can't be enforced.

However, while the inability of banks to foreclose on a mortgage or for a litigant to demonstrate adequate standing in a civil suit can provide two excellent examples of what the book is proposing for pushing back on a healthcare bill, the losses suffered in the two examples pale by comparison to what the healthcare industry would have at risk. That's because the losses associated with our two examples are local and disconnected from the market as a whole. A bank can simply find the documents it needs to foreclose on a particular mortgage and then refile. Furthermore, the lack of standing in a civil case only applies to that one particular case. However, not so for our disputed healthcare bill. Here, our push-back threatens to undercut the entire healthcare billing system with no solution in sight. Where our two examples carry very limited risk and cost, our push-back on a healthcare bill requires the disclosure of the very information the American Healthcare System has to keep secret. Information that by its very nature would disclose the disconnect between the system's Provider Agreements and the "Big Lie" – information that would lay bare the rationing of healthcare and the System's fraudulent billing.

There is one last point that needs to be made. Change in America is most commonly led by some financial change that drives the market to change. So if you need a greater justification for paying no more than what the American Healthcare System can "PROVE" is owed on a bill, please take comfort in knowing that by standing up for the explanation we are owed on a healthcare bill, you are striking a blow for responsible change in the entire American Healthcare System, i.e., change that we all need and want!

Please see the Appendix at the back of the book for specific examples of how to dispute an in-network healthcare bill.

Make your Response "PROMPT," Polite and Written

Please remember that when you decide to dispute a healthcare bill, you are, first and foremost, working to build a responsible defense for any attempts to enforce the bill. This means that anything other than a "PROMPT," respectful and responsible reply to a bill will be playing directly into the System's playbook.

As in any legal matter, a failure to reply "PROMPTLY" will create a wide open door for whoever sent the bill – a wide open door to request a court ordered judgement demanding you pay the bill. Furthermore, emotional arguments that a bill is too high, or you simply can't afford to pay it, can only lead down the rabbit hole the System has created to ensure they win and you lose. Right or wrong, the U. S. economic system allows a business to pretty much charge whatever they want and then have the courts enforce the bill. So, bitching about the pricing or the total cost is likely to be of little value, unless you are only looking for a discount on a bill – a pursuit far better taken up outside a courtroom.

One thing you can be absolutely sure of is that any large healthcare bill will have miles of indecipherable computer print-outs to support it. However, don't be fooled. The printouts that a provider or the System might be willing to share with you will only show their standard prices. Which will be of no particular value on their own. What you "NEED" are the standard prices and the discounted prices that: 1.) Your insurance company has negotiated, 2.) You are owed under the terms of the Provider Agreement for your plan and 3.) The provider is contractually "barred" from disclosing.

So, please believe me when I say that arguing pricing, or charges for items you claim you never received, is almost certainly a losing proposition. These are arguments that lead directly to where the System wants to take us. To bury us in a technical morass of paper, medical terminology and electronic data where the provider and the System hold all the cards. A morass of confusing back and forth geared to run out the clock on our ability to properly and legally dispute a bill.

What we want to do instead, is to take the provider or bill collector to a world where they dare not go, i.e., a world where it's "Cheaper to eat it." We want to take them to a world where the information that the Law requires is simply beyond the ability of a provider or bill collector to provide or disclose, or the risk of providing it is just too great.

What to "Include"

The following is a list of suggested items to include in a written response to an in-network healthcare bill. The intent of the items to put whoever sent the bill fully on notice that you are disputing both the accuracy and the appropriateness of the bill.

1.) The provider is to begin by acknowledging the inappropriateness of the claim that you owe whatever your plan or insurance fails to pay because the terms of their Provider Agreement say the very opposite.

2.) They are to itemize your bill by identifying all the products and services that they claim you received and that are included in the bill.

3.) The Itemized bill is to provide both their standard "Chargemaster prices and the discounted in-network prices that their Provider Agreement entitles you to receive.

4.) They are to include your "plan's" decisions on coverage for each item in the itemized bill, because you cannot be billed for an item of necessary healthcare regardless of whether the plan has denied coverage for the item, per the terms of their signed Provider Agreement.

5.) They are to justify each item charged to you as a copay, deductible or co-insurance based on their inability to bill you for necessary healthcare.

6.) They are to demonstrate compliance with the multiple provisions in their Provider Agreement that contractually bar them from billing you when your "plan" fails to pay for necessary healthcare.

7.) And lastly, they are to acknowledge the distinct difference between your insurer's contractual right to deny coverage, and the in-network provider's contractual obligation to deliver "All" necessary healthcare (even when contractually barred from billing the insurer or you).

Mail the Request to the "Healthcare Provider"

Your greatest chance for successfully disputing an in-network healthcare bill will come through written correspondence with the provider that sent the bill. After all, it's their bill, and it certainly won't be your insurance company or plan that forces a bill into collection. In fact, you can be confident that your insurer and plan will be staying as far away from any unpaid bill or collection process as they can get.

I should add that in recent years providers have shown a far greater interest in participating directly in the collection process. Rather than selling an unpaid debt to a collection agency for pennies on the dollar, providers are increasingly finding ways to pursue their own collections. However, you can be pretty certain they won't be doing it in their own name. That's because the majority of states require debt collectors to be licensed. But that won't stop a provider from creating their own, separate and licensed collection agency. The money is just too big!

Between 2009 and 2018, Maryland hospitals alone filed 145,746 medical debt lawsuits to pursue $268,711,620 from patients. On the surface, the $268,711,620 is a really big number and one just too big to be written off. However, it was only 4.7 percent of the hospitals' total net income for that period of time and a debt that the hospitals could have easily written off rather than file 145,746 separate lawsuits. I site these numbers to demonstrate just how aggressive the American Healthcare System has become in pursuing an unpaid bill. Bills that totaled only 4.7 percent of the Maryland hospital's net income, when their executive compensation was 46.6 percent of that same net income.

So, "please", focus on the fact that an unpaid healthcare bill isn't likely to go away on its own. **Focus on taking your insurer, plan, in-network provider or collection agency where they dare not go.** Focus on making them comply with the requirements of the FDCPA and CFPB by disclosing information they dare not disclose. Write to whoever sent the bill within 30-days of receiving it and: 1.) Formally dispute the accuracy and appropriateness of the bill, and 2.) Politely "SQUEEZE" them for answers they simply can't provide.

Copy Your "Insurer" on All Letters to the Provider

An in-network provider's greatest vulnerability is having to provide an explanation of a bill. Because, the confidentiality provisions of their Provider Agreement bar any such disclosure. So, by copying your insurer, or plan, on your request for information under the provisions of the FDCPA and CFPB, you alert the insurer to a potential breach of the confidentiality provisions of their Provider Agreement. And, you alert the provider to the likelihood that your insurer will be watching for any such a breach. Which is exactly where we want to put the provider and your insurer. In short, we want to create a true "Catch 22" that skewers the American Healthcare System on its own petard!

Stay Focused on an "Understandable Explanation"

I've had a long career doing many different things in life. One of the greatest successes I can claim is seldom, if ever, losing a fight. However, this is not to say I'm tough, smart or even clever. I simply learned early in life how to win. **You take your opponent where they can't afford to go.** You force them to fight on your terms, and in this case, you force your opponent into a position where it simply makes more sense to abandon the bill and walk away. The position of **"It's cheaper to eat it!"**

The beauty of the approach is that we are only asking for the explanation that the law affords us and the CFPB has stated we need to ask. Consequently, there is no downside or risk in asking or disputing a bill. After all, we aren't refusing to pay. We are simply asking for an explanation of a bill, so we can be assured it's accurate and appropriate. And, God knows, a large healthcare bill comes with no such explanation. In fact, the provider sending a large healthcare bill will almost certainly claim to have left out all that detailed information to avoid "burdening" us with it.

The Importance of "Medically Necessary" Care

Back when the Insurance industry wrote their Provider Agreements, they defined "coverage" as all the "Medically Necessary" care you and I would need. It was just that simple. If our doctor said we needed it, it was "Medically Necessary" and automatically qualified for coverage.

Fortunately, that simple contractual structure for coverage has never changed when it comes to defining what we are owed from our health insurance. **Which means that as long as our doctor prescribes the care we need as "Medically Necessary," we are "CONTRACTUALLY" owed both the care and the** cost of the care. Therefore, the only question allowed "CON-TRACTUALLY" is whether our "insurer" agrees to cover and pay for the care, or the in-network provider has to provide it for free. - - - Literally, a petard of the insurance industry's own making.

What about My "Deductible"

An in-network hospital or other healthcare provider that sends us a bill is not likely to know the amount of our Deductible, let alone what we may have already paid to satisfy it. In fact, it's far more likely that the only indication of what we owe on a Deductible will be buried in what our plan fails to pay on a particular bill. This will make separating what we supposedly owe on a deductible from our insurer's decisions on coverage all but impossible. Furthermore, while the language in some Provider Agreements attempts to provide some distinction between these different denials of coverage, there are numerous other provisions in the Agreements that out-an-out bar a provider from ever billing us for "Necessary Healthcare" – no exceptions allowed – deductible or no deductible. The uncovered portion of our bill simply becomes **"ONE"** big and inseparable failure to pay for the "Necessary Healthcare" that is guaranteed to us by the terms of our insurer's Provider Agreements.

> *"In no event, including but not limited to non-payment by Insurance Company, Insurance Company's insolvency or breach of this agreement, shall Provider, one of its subcontractors, or any of its employees or independent contractors bill, charge, collect a deposit from, seek compensation, remuneration or reimbursement from, or have any recourse against an Enrollee or persons other than the insurance company acting on behalf of Enrollee for Covered Services provided pursuant to this Agreement."*
>
> And
>
> *"Should Insurer determine a requested course of treatment is not Medically Necessary or Appropriate and Provider nonetheless provides that treatment,*

155

Provider shall not bill or charge Insurer or the insured Patient for any related costs associated with that denied admission or care."

Please understand, I'm not saying that, at least in principal, we won't owe something in the way of a deductible, co-insurance or co-pay as spelled-out in our healthcare plan. What I am saying is that, because of the misrepresentation and out-and-out fraud in the System, what we might owe on a Deductible for a particular in-network healthcare bill is an argument I just don't think a provider is going to want to make. After all, the very same disclosures required by the FDCPA and the CFPB will apply regardless of whether our insurer's denial of coverage is for a deductible, co-insurance or any other failure to pay for the care we need. Furthermore, we very much want it that way, because you and I don't want any part of having to identify the various failures for denying coverage on a bill. We want to leave that chore solely in the hands of the provider that sent the bill and <u>can't afford to disclose the information</u>.

And, What about My "Credit Score"

One of the first things I am generally asked when describing the book's approach to a healthcare bill is ***"What about my credit score"***? Won't my credit score be damaged if I don't pay my bill?

The good news is that it's not likely to happen. Quoting from Bulletin 2022-01: Medical Debt Collection and Consumer Reporting Requirements from the U. S. Consumer Financial Protection Bureau: 1.) Credit Reporting Agencies (CRAs) *"shall - - - assure maximum accuracy of the information concerning the individual about whom the report relates,"* 2.) CRAs shall *"establish written procedures on the accuracy and integrity"* of their reporting 3.) CRAs are *"required to conduct reasonable and timely investigations of consumer disputes to verify the accuracy of furnished information,"* and 3.) *"The Bureau will closely review the practices of those engaged in collecting and reporting medical debt"* and *"will hold CRAs accountable for failing to comply."*

Virtually no healthcare provider or debt collector is going

to report a failure to collect on a bill to a credit agency if the accuracy of the bill has been properly disputed under the provisions of the FDCPA and the recommendations of the CFPB. In fact, the three dominant reporting agencies have agreed "NOT" to accept such a report if the debt is less than 180 days old. This is more than enough time to subject a bill to the provisions of the FDCPA and CFPB. In addition, once you have subjected a bill to those provisions, "NO" action can be taken to enforce the bill until the required information is provided. In essence, any and all effort to enforce a bill is effectively frozen dead in its tracks preventing even the ability to report an unpaid bill as a bad debt. Even better, the CFPB invites you to report any failure to comply with these guidelines to: (https://www.consumerfinance.gov/complaint/).

No, I am not suggesting you use these quotes to dispute a healthcare bill. What I am saying is that **the CFPB has formally stated it is very aware that healthcare bills are rife with errors and that the Bureau will enforce against** *"any false representation of the character, amount or legal status of any debt."* What that means to this non-attorney is that if a provider or debt collector reports a bill as an unpaid debt to a Credit Reporting Agency or Service, after being informed that you are disputing the accuracy of the bill and requesting the information required to prove the accuracy and appropriateness of the bill, the provider or debt collector is violating the law and should be reported to the CFPB.

Summarizing How to "Dispute" a Healthcare Bill

While the book is aimed at explaining the general workings of the American Healthcare System and its "Big Lie," a complete understanding of the System, or your supposed health insurance, isn't needed to successfully dispute an in-network healthcare bill. All that is really needed is to: 1.) Immediately dispute the **accuracy** and **appropriateness** of a bill in a written letter to whoever sent the bill, 2.) Make the letter as friendly as possible, while requesting an understandable explanation of the bill as require by the FDCPA and CFPB, 3.) Send a copy of the letter to your plan/insurer, 4.) Make items 1, 2, and 3, the focus of your efforts to escape the System's "Big Lie," and 5.) View all other efforts to dispute a bill to be of secondary importance.

See the Appendix at the back of the book for suggestions on letters to use for disputing an in-network healthcare bill.

Chapter IX

Restore a man to his health,
his purse lies open to thee
Robert Burton

A Few Last Words on "Disputing" a Bill

There are a number of things that have become far too obvious about the American Healthcare System: 1.) The cost of healthcare has shown a steady increase as a percent of GDP for the past 20 years; 2.) There is "NO" reason to believe this trend will change; 3.) There is every reason to believe the American Healthcare System will shift more and more of these rising costs onto you and me; and 4,) These rising costs can be counted on to drive the U. S. Healthcare System to get increasingly creative in rationing the healthcare we receive.

Yes, there will be tinkering around the edges of the System. And, yes there will be a host of promises to make the System better. However, the bottom line is that the U. S. Healthcare System has become far too big to allow a major course correction. So, you and I are going to have to live with the System we have, i.e., a System steeped in fraudulent bills designed to pick our pocket, while lining the System's pockets with gold. So sad to say! But, I defy anyone with knowledge of the System to prove me wrong.

The one thing that just might change this dark forecast is the financial disruption that folks like you and I can create by simply disputing the System's indefensible and fraudulent healthcare bills under the provisions of the FDCPA and the CFPB. But, I'm getting too optimistic, because such a change would require a huge disruption of the System. In fact, I only mention it as a means of justifying the approach the book is suggesting. Because, while the approach and the justification are real, the System and its big money can be counted on to fight any significant change tooth and nail.

However, just as long as it's only a few of us pushing back on a healthcare bill, the System will simply conclude it's *"cheaper to eat it"* and move on – to simply cancel our bill and shift the efforts of the System to fleecing someone else. However, I will argue that if enough of us ever choose to no longer allow ourselves to be fleeced, there will come a time when choosing to eat a bill will no longer be a viable option for the System. That will be a time when the "Big Lie" is so well understood that the System will have to both seek and accept meaningful change.

Hopefully, if that day ever comes, the book will have played some role in providing the American People with the understanding they need to drive that change – a change that hopefully makes the American Healthcare System far more honest, respectful of individual patient needs, and accountable solely to the medical "judgement" of an attending physician (our doctor).

While there is much within the healthcare system that can and should be open for honest discussion and debate, there can never be any justification for the dishonesty and outright fraud that dominates the American Healthcare billing system.

....

Chapter X

Your individual needs must "__capitulate__
to the needs of the community:"
Mark Bertolini, CEO of Aetna

Where U.S. Healthcare is Headed
Setting the Table

As we said earlier, the future we are being herded toward is all too obvious. Doctors who are no longer our own personal physician, medications designed to provide a lifetime of monthly payments to the pharmaceutical industry, mega-hospitals owned by corporate holding companies more driven by the stock market than community service, and computerized billing systems so complex that a Certified Public Accountant can't verify the accuracy or appropriateness of a hospital bill. After all, what Public Accountant is going to be allowed to see a hospital's Provider Agreement?

Yes, we are assured time and again that the changes we are seeing in the American Healthcare System are aimed at improving our access to affordable healthcare. The underlying argument being that the changes bring greater efficiency, and with greater efficiency comes lower costs, i.e., greater access to affordable healthcare for you and me.

But, wait a minute! How come I can't get an appointment to see my doctor in under three weeks? How come it's getting harder to even identify "my" doctor in a practice of five or six doctors? How come when I do get an appointment to see my doctor, I am more and more likely to see a nurse practioner rather than my doctor? And, how come the time I do get to spend with whoever I see in the doctor's office is getting shorter and far more superficial in terms of addressing my healthcare needs?

Unhappy with my use of the word superficial? Well, ask anyone old enough to remember what a yearly physical examination used to include. I won't bore you with all the details, but as one old enough to remember those exams and having had them routinely as a Navy pilot and then as a DuPont employee, a yearly physical was a "VERY" complete review of your health. It routinely included testing for vision, hearing, lung capacity, a chest x-ray, the heart under stress, and all the way down to an examination for flat feet. In short, a doctor and the System took the time required to take a close look at our health. But, not anymore! The yearly physical has been reduced to little more than our height, weight, temperature, blood pressure, a blood test, answering a few simple questions, and then spending a few minutes with a doctor – a very few minutes.

The comparison couldn't be more striking. Where the yearly physical was once a detailed determination of an individual's actual health, it's now little more than checking a few boxes to show that we've had one. But, boy has this ever improved the efficiency of these physicals! That's because, the primary factor in determining efficiency is cost. - - - It will always be cheaper to avoid looking and kick the cost of whatever might be missed down the road to some future time and "payer."

Over the past couple of months I have had the misfortune of experiencing two very personal examples of just how costly this move to "not look too closely" can be. The first was when I had to rush my wife to the hospital and was told she was suffering from congestive heart failure. Three days later the hospital discharged her with instructions to see her cardiologist – a visit that took an unbelievable three weeks to schedule. And, a delay that caused the cardiologist to ask for another blood test. So back to the hospital we went for what we were told was just another routine blood test. However, it was a blood test that proved to be anything but routine. It was a test that saved her life, because she wasn't suffering from congestive heart failure, she was bleeding to death internally. In fact, if we hadn't gone back to the hospital by mere happenstance, Angie would have almost certainly died in her sleep that night. The hospital had simply failed to look beyond the most obvious problem of congestive heart failure when they discharged her from the hospital. The old Treat-em and Street-em operating at its very best.

The end result was that my wife didn't have a heart problem. She had a serious internal bleeding problem that was largely caused, and certainly made critical, by the heart medication she was on.

The second example had a far worse outcome in that my good friend Bill died from essentially the very same "lack of looking" that had nearly cost Angie her life. I had met Bill for one of our routine breakfasts and commented that he looked drawn and weak. He explained that he had lost 40-pounds and had a very large black and blue spot that essentially covered the entire side of his upper body. He further explained that he was working with his doctor, but was caught-up in a cycle of three weeks to schedule a visit, followed by a week or two to get a test and then another one or two weeks to schedule a return visit with his doctor.

I told him that the condition he was describing shouldn't be allowed to drag on and that he needed to put himself in the hospital where the testing would be immediate and there would be doctors 24x7 dedicated to getting him the care he needed, which is exactly what he did. He admitted himself through the emergency room at one of the most prestigious hospitals in the country. So, I honestly thought he was in good shape – I thought he was assured of getting the care he needed. - - - Three days later he was discharged and back home feeling somewhat better – but, still without learning what was really wrong. He had simply been discharged and advised to see his doctor for any additional care he "MIGHT" need.

My friend solved the 3-weeks needed to schedule an appointment with his doctor by having to be airlifted back to the hospital where he died never knowing what was wrong. In fact, when I saw his doctor, a doctor Bill and I had shared for more than thirty-years, the doctor's first words to me were, *"Did I know what Bill had died from?"* I said the hospital had discharged him far too quickly without ever determining what was wrong. The doctor replied *"No No, that can't be right, because Bill died in the hospital."* Making it blatantly obvious that Bill's doctor had never been informed, let alone consulted, on Bill's first admission to the hospital. - - - So much for the confidence we are supposed to have in the System's ability to replace "OUR" doctor with System's computer management system and their ever-more "efficient" Treat-em and Street-em approach to hospital admissions.

This reluctance to look beyond the immediate care needed is a growing reality in the American Healthcare System's pursuit of ever-greater efficiency. Not because I say it is, but because the math says it has to be. That's because Healthcare "efficiency" is simply a mathematical comparison of the cost of our healthcare to what the System actually delivers – the System, of course, claiming that the quality of care remains unchanged.

However, let's take a closer look at the math of "efficiency" to get a better picture of where we are headed. We can start by acknowledging that the cost of healthcare is rising at an unacceptable rate, i.e., the prices we pay for healthcare. The proof of this is everywhere. So, to increase "efficiency," the System has to reduce the stuff it delivers. Therefore, they have to cut what they deliver faster than the rising cost (prices) of healthcare. The math simply won't allow anything less.

Which brings us back to the problem that Angie and Bill faced in the hospital. Because there is no less efficient or more costly time spent in a hospital than the time it takes to fully diagnosis a patient. Furthermore, any failure to fully diagnosis a patient's needs will invariably get lost in the data.

A patient enters a hospital, as Bill did, and the records will clearly show that a problem was identified and properly treated. The fact that the patient later died was simply outside the hospital's best efforts to save them. Case closed, with no looking back to determine what was missed or anything that could hurt the System's pursuit of ever-greater efficiency.

Furthermore, the determination of efficiency is on a national basis. Making what was missed on an individual diagnosis like Angie and Bill even more remote and untraceable. Therefore, the System can improve the national efficiency of healthcare, while ignoring the very opposite when it comes to the care you and I receive as an individual.

All of which can only translate to a future with less and less individual healthcare for you and me from an American Healthcare System increasingly driven to "NOT" look too closely in order to increase the "efficiency" of the System, i.e., to simply Treat-em and Street-em! Or for the less cynical – to Greet-em, Treat-em and Street-em (the System's more caring words not mine). Furthermore, to do it while claiming that having a doctor spend less time with each of us is better for the System, because it frees doctors to serve an ever greater number of patients. The very thing Bill's doctor cited for preventing him from properly serving Bill and his other patients.

Of course, the real driver behind the loss of a doctor's ability to serve us isn't efficiency. It's money – BIG MONEY! Big money that argues the System has no choice but to cut the care we receive and certainly the care we get from our doctor.

The acceptable patient load for a doctor has long been viewed as something less than 1000 patients. Because that's the calculated number of patients that a doctor can see by working 8 hours a day, 5 days a week and for 52 weeks out of a year, i.e., the maximum number of patients a doctor can conceivably serve. However, the number of patients being cited as the appropriate goal based on efficiency and the financial needs of the System is between 2500 and 3000.

So, how does the American Healthcare System get from a maximum of 1000 patients to a goal of 3000? How do we take a doctor who can't see more than 1000 patients by working full-time, to accepting 3000 patients? After all, it's very akin to asking an engineer to supervise 3000 projects, or an attorney to handle 3000 cases. Both laughable and completely unattainable goals. So, what's the difference here? How can our doctor and the American Healthcare System do something that any other field of equally responsible licensed professionals can't possibly do?

They eliminate the liability of a doctor and the System for what gets missed – they institute a strategy of not looking too closely. In other words, they cook the books.

When an engineer has a bridge collapse, or an attorney makes a mistake in representing a client, the failure is typically obvious and there for anyone who would care to look. Furthermore, the records are, if anything, overly complete, permanent and designed to ensure that a single individual is responsible for every significant decision made.

However, we are seeing something quite different in our new and evolving American Healthcare System. By spreading doctors over a greater and greater number of patients, the System gets to spread the delivery of healthcare over a greater and greater number of people other than a doctor and certainly not a single doctor. Most important, the System gets to spread the diagnosis of what's wrong across this same greater and greater number of doctors and support staff.

While the engineer and the attorney have their response to a problem fully defined and documented, our more "efficient" doctor is accountable only for what gets identified when a patient enters a hospital. Furthermore, the substitution of computers and staffing for a doctor's time, along with spreading the treatment of a patient across a team of doctors, has diluted even this limited liability. In other words, there is no one person or doctor accountable for what gets missed, i.e., no doctor accountable for what got missed with Angie and Bill.

The role of our family doctor, or more properly a PCP, has changed drastically over the past ten years as physicians have struggled to manage immense numbers of patients and still build a meaningful relationship with those in their care. After all, how can a doctor be expected to actually know a patient when the patient is no more than one out of 3000 or so patients that he or she is expected to see and treat?

Regardless of how much data gets crammed into an individual's computer file, or how many are add to a doctor's staff, a PCP simply can't know 3000 patients in the way we expect from our doctor. We have effectively become a stranger to our PCP, while being led to increasingly accept this as the normal doctor-patient relationship.

However, the strain of all this change has been anything but normal and reasonable. For, while the doctor of the past could determine the appropriate number of patients for his or her practice, the doctor of today has no such freedom. The typical PCP of today is an employee of a large corporate healthcare provider and told what he or she has to accept as an appropriate number of patients. In fact, the PCP's corporate employer will almost certainly have a computer management system capable of tracking every working moment of the doctor's day to ensure the most efficient use of the doctor's time. Time now stripped of both the rewarding personal relationships doctors once shared with their patients and the technical challenge of participating in the advancement of medical science. Two elements of the job that once drove doctors to view their careers as rewarding beyond any direct compensation. Their time and career now dictated far more by the clock and an increasingly complex healthcare bureaucracy with no relief in sight.

So can there be any surprise that a primary reason PCPs are citing for leaving their practice is burnout. One out of every five doctors is expected to retire in the next two years.

Making this problem even worse is that the United States has an aging population that can only create a growing demand for healthcare – expensive and complex healthcare. Adding to this is the remarkable growth in technology that is rapidly expanding the field of expensive care rather than creating less costly treatments. In fact, care that didn't exist only a few years ago is now routinely viewed as necessary. Where our parents suffered with knees and hips that grew increasingly painful with age, the elderly now expect to have them replaced. However, the $50,000 bill our parents never saw is now an everyday expense in today's healthcare system. In addition, where our parents would have taken the occasional aspirin for pain, our generation takes at least one prescription drug a day, with 20 percent hooked on taking more than five.

The simple math of all this says that the cost of healthcare can only increase, not decrease or even level off. Furthermore, it's this same inescapable math that has the American Healthcare System focused on rationing our healthcare under the guise of pursuing ever-greater "efficiency." All the while jacking prices through the roof to drive profits when the financial security of working families has never been under greater pressure, and our aging population will need increasingly higher levels of expensive healthcare. It's a reality that is even starker if we add in the difference between what Medicare pays for healthcare and what our private health insurance pays for the very same products and services – a difference that can be as much as 1,000 percent. In fact, a Rand study of 25 states found that hospital prices across the board averaged 241 percent above what Medicare pays for the same care.

However, do we see Washington taking steps to correct this imbalance in pricing? Do we see Washington calling for less expensive new construction in healthcare facilities? Do we see Washington informing us that Medicare Advantage is every bit as guilty of rationing healthcare as the insurance provided by an employer? No we do NOT! We don't see any of the reasonable steps being taken that would reduce the cost of healthcare or to even inform us of the rationing taking place within the American Healthcare System. What we see is Washington adopting the term "efficiency" for what is clearly rationing, the loss of our doctor, and the growth of uncontrolled pricing – rationing being a radio-active term and an anathema in party politics. Furthermore, the loss of our doctor is being sold to us much like the proverbial frog in a slowly heating pot of water, while the out of control rise in healthcare pricing is justified as a necessary inducement for innovation.

Unfortunately, the pursuit of greater "efficiency" in healthcare conveys the appearance of the American Healthcare System and federal government headed in the right direction. Both simply working for better management of the nation's healthcare delivery system in order to provide ever-greater access to affordable healthcare. All the while leaving: 1.) Providers free to raise their prices to offset the insurance industry's growing cuts in coverage, 2.) Insurers free to respond to these rising prices by raising the cost of our health insurance and 3.) Both free to ration our healthcare to grow their bottom line – and all while claiming to be doing nothing more than pursuing the intent of Congress for controlling the cost of healthcare.

The bottom line is that what we are being told about the need for greater "efficiency" is a mere parsing of words for the creation of ever-greater rationing of the healthcare we receive. In fact, it's a bit like measuring the efficiency of an automatic car wash. We can get higher efficiency by simply increasing the speed of the cars passing through the carwash. But, does that mean the cars will be just as clean as they were at the slower speed. We already know that a custom wash by a skilled individual will take longer and cost more, but is certain to deliver a higher quality and more extensive cleaning. Like a detailed cleaning of the interior. However, the difference in cost is on the order of $10 for the automatic carwash and $100 for a custom carwash.

So, the economic premise of the automatic carwash industry is that you and I can be made to accept a lower quality carwash for a lower price. All well and good when we are talking about the looks of our car. However, not so easily accepted when it's our healthcare and <u>we aren't being given a choice</u>.

In the case of the carwash, that high quality custom service is still available for those willing to pay for it. But, not for healthcare. Here we are being forced to accept the speeding-up of the system that increasingly strips us of the time we need and have every right to expect from our doctor and the American Healthcare System – along with the time required to determine what was really wrong with Angie and Bill.

This drive for ever-greater "efficiency" is a direct indicator of where the American Healthcare System is headed, because it's the natural evolution of every business under American capitalism. Furthermore, this drive for ever-greater efficiency has been the magic behind the growth of the U. S. economy.

Large flat screen TVs are a perfect example. Where a small black and white TV once cost more than a middle class family could afford, the behemoth color TVs of today are routinely purchased by even the most average working class family.

Unfortunately, the factors driving the cost of healthcare far outweigh what can be achieved through competition and efficiency. Technology is adding new layers of cost to healthcare at an unprecedented rate, and the growing scarcity of doctors can only accelerate the rise in the cost to see a doctor.

The truth is that we aren't even trying to develop cheaper or more affordable cures for things like the common cold. That's because the greater profits lie in treating terminal cancer, MS or other currently untreatable disease. These are treatments that come with patent rights and with years of uncontested pricing and profits. All driving the cost of healthcare not only up, but up at an ever increasing rate.

The truth is that we can't escape some form of healthcare rationing. We can't be giving new hearts to 85-year olds, miracle drugs that can costs $35,000 a month for the rest of a person's life, or a bone marrow transplant for cancer when the patient is terminally ill with some other disease. We simply can't ignore what these costs would do to the American Healthcare System. Or more simply put, we can't afford to pay for every "perceived" healthcare need in the country.

Even countries that offer universal healthcare don't provide all the care everyone might need or want. They provide a reasonable standard of care so that everyone gets the same level of healthcare. - - - It's called rationing. And, the United States is well into it regardless of what you and I are told. However, the countries with universal healthcare don't have providers and insurers profiting from this necessary rationing. Furthermore, they are open and honest about its existence while our leaders both hide it and openly lie about its very existence.

The indisputable truth is that rationing has been an everyday reality in the United States for many years. A fact unanimously confirmed by the U. S. Supreme Court's in Pegram v. Hedrich. However, in spite of this Supreme Court ruling, the insurance industry, our government and most particularly our politicians refuse to acknowledge what the Supreme Court found so obvious. Instead, we are constantly encouraged to turn a blind eye to the rationing in the America Healthcare System, along the misrepresentation and outright fraud used to drive the obscene level of profit in the American Healthcare System.

Although it's a bit dated and stated earlier in the book, it worth stating a second time because it characterizes the state of the American Healthcare System so well.

Steven Brill did a masterful job of describing the U. S. Healthcare System in the March 4, 2013 addition of Time magazine. According to Brill, our "PRIVATE" U. S. Healthcare System has become *"a uniquely American gold rush — from Stanford, Conn., to Marlton, N.J., to Oklahoma City . . . ."* Brill goes on to report that *"the American health care market has transformed tax-exempt nonprofit hospitals into the town's most profitable business and largest employers, often presided over by the region's most richly compensated executives."* The New York Times, in a lead article that same year (May 18, 2013) provides us with another excellent example of this transformation. The Times reported that in 2007 the Bayonne Medical Center was a bankrupt hospital in *"a faded blue-collar town 11 miles from Midtown Manhattan."* Today that same hospital charges among the highest rates in the country and its profits have "soared."

However, we don't have to rely on the words of a reporter to understand the profitability of our "PIVATE" Healthcare System. We can see for ourselves the same thing that drove Steven Brill to write his article for *Time*. While visiting Houston, Mr. Brill noticed a group of glass skyscrapers lighting up the evening sky. *"The scene looked like Dubai,"* reported Brill. It was, in fact, the Texas Medical Center with 280 buildings sitting on nearly 1,300 acres. It's one of Houston's largest employers. I had the same experience while attending a conference at the University of Pennsylvania Medical Center. Stretching out over untold blocks of downtown Philadelphia and boasting the most modern and expensive construction, the size and grandeur of the facility was amazing. In fact, it literally screamed money and power.

However, this is just the obvious part of what has become the most dominant part of our national economy. Representing roughly twenty percent of the nation's GDP, the healthcare industry will generate roughly four trillion dollars of revenue in the coming year. And, to ensure this flood of money keeps pouring in, the healthcare industry is spending roughly $5.4 billion a year (that's billion with a "B") lobbying Congress, as compared to roughly $2 billion for the defense and aerospace industries, and $1.5 billion for the oil and gas interests. So, we can be confident that the healthcare industry is doing its level best to keep the money pouring in. However, like all big business, success is measured by growth rather than current earnings alone. Consequently, we can be equally confident that our nation's healthcare leaders aren't lobbying Congress to maintain the status quo. They are lobbying for ever-greater power to ration healthcare, while raising the cost of the healthcare we can't do without.

And, what is Congress' response to all this? We hear it time and again. What we need to achieve this greater efficiency is "greater competition." But, look at any big city. Do we see anything even close to this growing competition in healthcare? What we see is just the opposite. For example, Philadelphia and the surrounding area is owned by Penn Medicine on the provider side, and Independence Blue Cross on the insurer side. Two corporate giants that simply aren't allowing any room for competition. And, it's only getting worse across the country as giants like these two buy up everything in sight to virtually eliminate competition, i.e., Steven Brill's *"American Gold Rush."*

Proof Positive of Where We're Headed

Fortunately, you don't have to take Steven Brill's word or mine for where American Healthcare System is headed. You don't even have to look to reporters or forecasts. Mark Bertolini, the former CEO of Aetna, took all the guesswork out of the issue during an in-depth interview he gave to Dylan Scott for *Governing* magazine a number of years ago. In fact, Mr. Bertolini was so clear and unambiguous in his statements that we have to believe that Aetna and the rest of the large players in the healthcare insurance market believe they have the future of the American Healthcare System well in hand.

To provide some context for Mr. Bertolini's comments, Aetna has more than forty million enrollees, one million providers under contract, and yearly revenue of more than thirty billion dollars a year. Furthermore, the future of this 160-year-old company depends on its ability to not just maintain its position in the healthcare market, but to grow its power and profits some three to five percent a year for as far as the eye can see. But, this just speaks to the corporate identity of Aetna. Because Aetna is owned by an even greater corporate giant, i.e., CVS Healthcare Systems.

But I digress. The key to understanding where our healthcare system is headed is Mr. Bertolini's insistence that the future of the U. S. Healthcare System must be built around what he calls *"population health management."* He describes it as a way to *"improve the health of the population in a way that provides a more valuable input into the economy of the country. So it would be an investment in productivity."* Mr. Bertolini goes on to say that Population Health Management *"would have a community based organization that would not only be a large employer in the economy but also a key provider of economic input."* And that our healthcare system would be *"a true popular health system . . . which would meet with the community and understand the ongoing demography, disease burden and trends."* It's a system where one's individual need for care *"would capitulate to the needs of that community over time."* He added that *"the outcome that we would measure is"* whether the *"economy is better off."*

I hate to break into Mr. Bertolini's thoughts, but isn't that the very heart of socialism? Where the individual needs that you and I have must take a backseat to the needs of the nation, i.e., **"CAPITULATE?"** Where do we find *"capitulate to the needs of the community"* in our nation's guarantee of Life, Liberty and the Pursuit of Happiness, or the Constitution's guarantee of individual rights? Where? Please tell me Mr. Bertolini, where? - - - But, back to Mr. Bertolini and his comments.

Mr. Bertolini further explained that he and Aetna, along with the other large insurers, have: 1.) The data necessary to understand *"how the system should be constructed,"* 2.) The *"technology"* to collect the necessary *"information"* on enrollees, and 3.) The *"financing capability to make sure that the investment is well handled."* It's a system where the American people would *"think of an insurance company . . . as a highly specialized bank"* that provides *"financing, risk management, reinsurance coverage . . . intellectual property, data and technology as the intelligence side of a health-care system."* Pardon me. But, if that isn't bold faced rationing I just don't know what is.

However, most telling was Mr. Bertolini's answer to Dylan Scott's question of *"Are you doing this somewhere?* He said yes, *"in China."* Mr. Bertolini went on to say that Aetna will be working with the Chinese government *"to set up this type system"* because they *"don't have the barriers there that we have here."* The Chinese, he added, *"don't have entrenched interests . . . to overcome,"* and, Aetna believes it can *"create a cresting wave phenomenon . . . that will allow us to try it here in the United States."*

As to what Mr. Bertolini forecasts for our doctors and hospitals, he was equally open and explicit. The new system will *"require us to go about our work differently. It's not a negotiation with providers over what to pay them, but a partnership with providers to understand what we're investing in and how we can both work together to make sure that investment achieves the maximum return."* And, ***"It really requires the providers to trust us in ways that they've never had to trust us."*** - - - To have our doctor ***"TRUSTING"*** the insurer over his or her own judgement on the care we need and should be allowed to receive.

Mr. Bertolini's statements were made a number of years ago and viewed by me at the time as an exaggeration of where we were headed. I honestly thought that the combination of common sense, established law and the U. S. Constitution would provide an insurmountable barrier to such a monumental revision of individual rights within and our free market economy and the American Healthcare System.

No more! Because as they say in the born again church, *"I have seen the light!"* I am seeing the very changes Mr. Bertolini described. - - - Like, trying to find a doctor willing to take the time to diagnosis what was wrong with my wife. The hospital discharging her when she was bleeding to death internally, and offering no more than the advice to see her doctor. Then having to go nose to nose with the hospital, when she was readmitted near death, to get them to make the most obvious decision needed to save her life. - - - Then there was seeing my dear friend Bill fail to get the care he needed at one of the nation's most prestigious hospitals. A situation where he was discharged without being diagnosed, and simply told to see his doctor, only to be airlifted back to the hospital where he subsequently died. - - - And, Bill's doctor of 30-years, along with Bill's family, never to be told what caused his death. - - - Having my brother die on the floor of a medical rehabilitation facility, because they refused to take him to the hospital where he could have been treated – a rehabilitation facility where the only doctor lived two hours away and was only required to visit the facility once every 60 days, but, a facility where the cost of my brother's care was substantially less than in the hospital. - - - A healthcare insurance company that delivered 17-pages of terms and conditions 2-weeks after the contract was signed and the insurer could expect the 17-pages to go undiscussed and simply filed away as just so much more paper. However, those 17-pages gave the insurer full control over the healthcare our employees could receive, without any liability for those decisions. - - - A system where Dr. Sree Chaguturu, CVS Healthcare Systems Chief Medical Officer declared *"Healthcare is broken,"* while CVS purchased Oak Street Health with 600 primary care doctors in over 180 locations for 10.6 billion dollars to broaden its control over the care you and I can receive from Dr. Chaguturu's broken healthcare system.

In short, I have truly been forced to, *"see the light!"* When Sandy died, it took me years of contentious litigation to get my hands on the internal records that showed how our insurer had overridden Sandy's doctor to deny the lifesaving care Sandy needed. But, that was 20-years ago. Furthermore, it was a time when insurers had to hide their overruling of a doctor and a time when I was absolutely convinced that the law and common sense would hold our insurer accountable for Sandy's death. In fact, it was a time when our insurer spent the better part of eight years in court denying that any such overruling of a doctor was even possible.

Now, fast forward to today. We not only have insurers overruling doctors, but doing it openly and making no bones about it. Where my doctor was once in private practice, he is now an employee of the System and subject to the policies and oversight of the System. In fact, he is an employee of the hospital system that refused to allow me to pay for Sandy's care. Now, add to that CVS's recent purchase of 900 doctors, and the picture really begins to take shape. Insurers are no longer twisting arms behind the scene to overrule a doctor, as they did in the case of my wife Sandy. The System now owns the doctor. The doctor having become little more than an employee forced to execute the decisions of the System – a system where *"the profit incentive to ration care"* goes *"to the very point of any health insurance"* (the opinion of U. S. Supreme Court in Pegram et al. v. Herdrich).

But, it gets even worse for us while getting far better for the System and their ability to ration healthcare. By acquiring ownership of both the doctors and the hospitals, the System has been able to completely redefine the role of a primary care physician, i.e. the one we have always look to as our very own family doctor. Quoting from numerous sources readily available on Goggle, *"Over the last 20+ years, the model for patient care in hospitals has changed"* – *"Primary care physicians no longer participate in the care provided by a hospital"* – *"A Primary Care Physician who will follow a patient into a hospital is VERY rare exception"* – *"Hospitals now have hospitalists who perform the role of your doctor in the hospital."*

Stating this as simply as I can, the System has managed to COMPLETELY separate our doctor (now defined as a Primary Care Physician or PCP) from all of the critical and <u>expensive</u> healthcare decisions made in a hospital.

I have said a number of times that the people responsible for the design of the American Healthcare System are very smart people. What I haven't said is that these are ethical people. Because, while the redefining of the System, along with redefining the role of our doctor, may have paved the way to Mr. Bertolini's forecast for the American Healthcare System, these changes can in no way be seen as ethical. In fact, they survive only through dishonesty and secrecy, as the laws that guarantee us "our" very own doctor and all the healthcare our doctor determines we need, are still very much in place. We just have to be concerned enough to understand our rights and refused to be rolled.

Mr. Bertolini's forecast may have become a reality for the nation. However, I see absolutely no reason why it has to become a reality for you and me, so long as we know our rights and aren't afraid to demand them rather than stand idly by as the American Healthcare System distorts the law to *"capitulate"* our right to receive necessary healthcare and ensures their *"investment achieves the maximum return."*

Mr. Bertoline, I have come to a point where I have to agree that your forecast was spot on. It has simply taken some very large and personal bumps in the road for me to *"See the light!"*

Disconnected by Power & Money

While Mr. Bertolini's forecast for the U. S. Healthcare System is extremely clear and concise, it can be condensed into far fewer words. Namely, *"We will be taking control of the nation's health care system, and the needs of the individual patient will have to take a backseat to the financial needs of the healthcare insurance industry, the American Healthcare System, and the nation."*

Therefore, like Mr. Bertolini, I feel I can be equally clear and concise in expressing my opinion on this future. Or, to express in plain English my view of where the System is headed, i.e., "No F---ing way!" Furthermore, my Republican Party and its conservative wing should be equally incensed by this future. Because, what Mr. Bertolini describes as the *"barriers"* to his plans for the American Healthcare System is what we commonly refer to as the U. S. Constitution, along with the word and spirit of this nation's laws. Unlike China, where the only individual right to care, that I am aware of, is the right to a speedy execution if you upset the government, this country is grounded in the inalienable rights of the individual – rights that emanate from the governed and not government – rights that cannot be cast aside or ignored for the convenience and profit of the participants in our private healthcare system.

Unless of course, we the people are dumb enough to let it happen.

The Reality We Face

Both the reality of Mr. Bertolini's forecast and the future of the American Healthcare System are there for all of us to see, if we just take the time to look. So much so that the most recent edition of a local Fishwrapper newspaper felt the need to opine on the state of the Healthcare System. *"Do all diagnostic procedures require pre-certification?"* Answer – *"No, only those you need."* - - - *"Can I get coverage for a pre-existing condition?"* Answer – *"Certainly, as long as you don't need any treatment."* - - - *"Will healthcare be any different in the next decade?"* Answer – *"No, but if you call right now, you might get an appointment by then."* - - - All so very true and right in front of us. But the Fishwrapper quote I like best of all is, *"I just joined a new HMO, how difficult will it be to choose the doctor I want?"* Answer – *"Just slightly more difficult than choosing your parents."*

And, then there was this year's meeting with the insurance representative that my wife and I use for our family business. Once again, we would have to choose from eight or so different plans, all significantly different from our existing plan. And, all so convoluted by changing co-payments, deductibles and the limits on coverage that I defy anyone to make a meaningful comparison of the plans we were offered for the coming year. It just isn't statistically possible, given the large number of variables that have to be considered – which can only mean that the confusion is by design, i.e., intentional. In fact, when I expressed my conclusion that the confusion was obviously intentional, the representative readily agreed with me. The plans were just beyond understanding. However, what was understandable was the insurer's steady march toward reducing coverage, while extending their control over the care and coverage our employees would be allowed to receive.

Chapter XI

....

*"There can be times when we are powerless
to prevent injustice, but there must never be
a time when we fail to protest"*
Elie Wiesel
Nobel Laureate & Holocaust Survivor

Wrapping Up
A Summary of the Book

Under our capitalistic system, companies can pretty much market whatever they choose. We not only allow it, we encourage it as an engine of growth for the economy. However, a healthcare insurance company's freedom to market a product can't void an individual's right to freely access the advice of his or her doctor and the care the doctor prescribes as "necessary" healthcare. This is an absolute in law, and, it's something no insurance company or plan can change regardless of what they claim or how they spin the terms and conditions of their supposed health insurance/plan. Furthermore, our right to receive the free healthcare guaranteed by the insurance industry's Provider Agreements can't be swept away by an insurance company or the fraudulent billing practices of an in-network provider – unless <u>you and I stand silently by and allow it to happen</u> <u>– and, unless we are content to become the sheep the American</u> <u>Healthcare System's "BIG LIE" is intent on fleecing!</u>

We are a nation of individual rights that just happen to include a contractual right to free healthcare when our insurer ignores the care prescribed by our doctor. And, given the rampant errors in healthcare billing, a fact repeatedly confirmed by the CFPB, our only concern should be: 1.) Our right to request and receive an understandable explanation of an in-network healthcare bill by formally disputing the bill under the provisions of the FDCPA, 2.) Making the request in writing within the 30-day window allowed by the Act, and 3.) Insisting that the explanation provide "proof" that the bill is accurate and appropriate per the recommendations of the CFPB, or that all efforts to collect the bill be terminated.

If the book does nothing more than to convince the reader to follow these three simple steps for pushing back on a healthcare bill, then the book will have fulfilled its mission and more than met the aspirations of the author.

Lastly

The author needs to remind readers that he is not an attorney, nor is he representing himself as an expert on the laws governing healthcare or insurance in the United States or any particular state. This book is solely an attempt to share what ten years of litigation and the death of Sandra Lobb, along with a number of other personal confrontations with the healthcare system, appear to have taught the author about the American Healthcare System and the insurance industry in particular. Therefore, anyone choosing to use the information or suggestions contained in the book needs to understand that: 1.) They are acting on their own without any warrantee or guarantee of results from the author, the book or the publisher, 2.) Any suggestions in the book, either inferred or direct, rest solely on the perceived obligation of an in-network provider or bill collector to provide an explanation of a bill as required by the Fair Debt Collection Practices Act, 3.) A billed individual do no more than offer to pay a bill in exchange for an explanation that verifies the accuracy and appropriateness of a bill, and 4.) Readers are advised to seek legal counsel prior to doing anything other than disputing the accuracy and apropriateness of a heathcare bill under the rights granted by the FDCPA and the recommendations of the CFPB.

And lastly, nothing in the book is to be interpreted as encouraging any form of litigation to clarify or challenge the insurance industry's use of Provider Agreements and/or the provisions contained in such agreements.

Chapter XII

....

The doctor begins to lose freedom - - - -
and from here it is only a short step to
dictating where he will go
                                    Ronald Reagan

Some Rules for the Road
Ways to Make the System "Work" for You

It's important to understand that there are two (2) fundamentally different types of health insurance in the country. The first is the private insurance supplied by an employer or purchased individually from an insurance company like Humana, Blue Cross, United Healthcare and a laundry list of others. The second is government insurance that comes in the form of Medicare, Medicaid, and Tricare. Only government insurance "guarantees" you the right to the care and coverage your doctor prescribes as necessary healthcare. All the private plans, including Medicare Advantage, restrict care and coverage to what the insurer decides you should be <u>allowed</u> to receive – Medicare Advantage being nothing more than a private insurance plan that Medicare purchases for an individual who chooses to receive a Medicare Advantage plan rather than the traditional form of Medicare. Consequently, Medicare Advantage plans are subject to all the misrepresentations, restrictions and outright fraud that the book has cited for private health insurance.

Government Health Insurance:
(Medicare, Medicaid and Tricare)
- Care and Coverage are "GUARANTEED" by Federal Law.
- All pertinent information is fully available.

Private Health Insurance: (Including Medicare Advantage)
- Care and Coverage are "RESTRICTED" by secret contracts. (Provider Agreements)
- Critical information is intentionally "NOT" available.

> Confirmed in AARP's June 2023 Bulletin and in Federal Rules that take effect Sept, 30, 2023.

The following suggestions are the rules of the road that the author uses to make the System work for himself and his family. They are simply what 20-years of study and experience has taught him about the American Healthcare System.

1.) Make your doctor an advocate for the care and coverage you need or get another doctor. Most important, find a doctor willing to go beyond the limits of a Primary Care Physician and serve all your healthcare needs. There are still a few out there and their value is well worth the time it takes to find them.

2.) If you have reason to be seriously concerned about your health or the health of a loved one (the loss of significant weight, a steady worsening of health, unexplained fatigue, pain or nausea, or a family doctor's failure to diagnose the problem), seriously consider entering a hospital where testing is immediate and a team of doctors will be focused on getting to the bottom of the problem. - - - However, <u>make absolutely certain that the hospital is focused on determining the root cause of what is wrong, and not simply treating the most obvious issue identified in the emergency room.</u>

3.) Make absolutely certain that the healthcare provider you use (doctor, hospital or Indian Chief) is under contract as an in-network provider with your "plan and insurer." An assurance that a hospital, clinic or healthcare provider "ACCEPTS" your insurance is completely misleading and only indicates a willingness to bill your plan while expecting you to pay whatever doesn't get covered.

4.) Familiarize yourself with the terms of the Provider Agreement in the Appendix and don't be afraid to share what you learn with the in-network providers you use. It has been my experience that professionals in the healthcare system feel every bit as trapped as we are and appreciate someone who has taken the time to understand the System.

5.) Ensure you have one doctor who is "clearly" in charge of your care rather than a team of doctors where no one doctor is responsible for the care you receive. Only then can you have accountability for what you receive. This is particularly important in a hospital, because the doctors will be working in shifts with no one doctor responsible for the care a patient receives.

6.) Never undergo an expensive operation or procedure without confirming that your doctor has ordered it as *"medically necessary"* care. It's your guarantee of coverage under the terms of your insurer's Provider Agreement.

7.) Consider giving an in-network hospital a brief letter at the time of admission stating that, as an in-network hospital, it's the hospital's responsibility to ensure that all the care you receive qualifies as in-network care, unless specifically approved in writing by you or your representative. This will eliminate your responsibility for any surprise out-of-network bills. This is particularly applicable when entering a hospital for surgery where the anesthesiologist will very likely be an out-of-network doctor looking to bill you directly and out-side of your insurance.

8.) Always insist on seeing a copy of an emergency room's "written" diagnosis.

9.) Remember that an emergency room is only required to stabilize a patient. The law does not require any treatment past stabilization of a patient's condition. Furthermore, an emergency room is likely to assign a single billing code for what is needed and then only address that problem before discharging you back to see your doctor, i.e., a family doctor who's revised role is to only treat the most basic healthcare needs.

10.) Never accept an out-of-network bill from someone working in an in-network hospital. They are a subcontractor of the hospital and need to bill the hospital not you. The only exception would be if you actually approved their participation in your care.

11.) ALWAYS remember that both the CARE and COVERAGE you are owed from your "plan" is the **medically necessary** healthcare your doctor prescribes, regardless of what your insurer or plan wants to claim. That's because your insurer's Provider Agreement is the only binding agreement on the care and coverage you are owed. And, it states that you are to receive ALL the "medically necessary" care your doctor prescribes with payment for the care to be negotiated SOLELY between the provider and your insurer.

12.) ALWAYS insist that your written responses to an in-network bill be made a permanent part of the provider's file.

13.) NEVER allow yourself to be drawn into a debate between your doctor's opinion and that of your insurer's doctor. Their doctor has "NO" legal standing in determining "necessary healthcare" for you. Only the attending doctor (your doctor) can make that determination. All an insurer's doctor is empowered to do is to contractually determine whether the insurer pays for the care prescribed by your doctor, or the in-network provider has to provide it for free.

14.) And, stating it one more time: The form you signed accepting financial responsibility for what your insurer fails to pay on an in-network bill of any type (doctor, hospital, clinic or Indian chief) is bogus, because the provider has surrendered the right to make such a claim by signing their Provider Agreement.

15.) And lastly, we will end this section and the book with an explanation to a question the book must have raised early on: Why would a healthcare insurer want to prevent you or me from paying for our own healthcare? - - - The answer is remarkably simple. It's to control (ration) the care we get. You see, if our insurer denies coverage, and we get the care by simply paying for it, we would create a prima facie claim for coverage and reimbursement. It would be a slam-dunk case in court. Doctors can only render "medically necessary" healthcare. And, since our doctor prescribed and rendered the care we received, it can only have been "medically necessary," AND care that is specifically <u>covered by our plan</u>. - - - So, it's just so much more efficient for our insurer or plan to ensure we never get the care and avoid the legal liability, i.e., liability that could literally bring down the roof on the entire American Healthcare System and its "<u>uniquely American Gold Rush</u>."

Appendix 1

Response to an In-network Healthcare Bill

Dear In-Network Provider;

I have received your bill and wish to get the matter settled as soon as possible. However, I am familiar with the billing restrictions in your Provider Agreement and the Consumer Financial Protection Bureau (CFPB) has found healthcare billing "rife" with error. Consequently, I am disputing the accuracy and appropriateness of your bill under the provisions of the Fair Debt Collection Practices Act and the recommendations of the CFPB, and requesting the following:

1. Please begin by acknowledging that I am "not" financially responsible for what my health insurance has failed to pay for the necessary healthcare I received, because: 1.) My "plan" is insurance in name only, 2.) You have contractually agreed to accept whatever my insurer pays for my necessary healthcare as payment in full, and 3.) You are contractually barred from billing me for such necessary healthcare, regardless of whether my insurer elects to cover the cost of the care.

2. Please provide an itemized bill that includes: 1.) Your undiscounted prices, and 2.) The discounted prices that I am entitled to receive and need to determine the accuracy of your bill.

3. Please provide my insurer's decisions on coverage for "each" item in your bill as these decisions are essential for determining the accuracy and appropriateness of the bill.

Please be advised that your failure to provide the requested information will be seen as an acknowledgement that you are unwilling or unable to validate your bill. Lastly, please ensure this letter becomes a permanent part of the file on bill.

Yours truly,

cc: Your Healthcare Insurer or Plan

Appendix 2

Follow-up Response #1

Dear In-Network Provider;

    I have received a second copy of your bill, but without the information I requested in disputing the accuracy and appropriateness of the bill. Consequently, I am attaching a copy of my earlier letter, and again requesting that information.

    Please ensure this and my earlier letter are made a permanent part of the file on the bill.

Yours truly,

cc: Your Healthcare Plan
     State Department of Insurance
     U. S. Consumer Financial Protection Bureau

Appendix 3

Follow-up Response #2

Dear In-Network Provider;

    I have received another copy of your bill, but once again without the information I have requested in disputing the bill, i.e., the information needed to validate the accuracy and appropriateness of the bill. So, I am attaching a copy of my earlier two letters, and again requesting that information.

    Once again, please ensure this letter becomes a permanent part of the file on the bill.

Yours truly,

cc: Your Healthcare Plan
      State Department of Insurance
      State Attorney General

Appendix 4

Follow-up Response #3

Dear In-Network Provider;
    (Or Collection Agency)

    I have received yet another copy of the attached bill and once again without the information needed to validate the accuracy and appropriateness of the bill as is my right under the provisions of the Fair Debt Collection Practices Act and the actions of the CFPB.

    Please note that your failure to provide this information can only be seen as **an unwillingness or inability to validate the bill**. Consequently, I will consider the matter closed unless I hear otherwise.

    Please make this letter a permanent part of your file on the bill, along with my earlier letters requesting such validation.

                          Yours truly,

cc: Your Healthcare "Plan"
      State Department of Insurance
      State Attorney General
      U. S. Consumer Financial Protection Bureau

Representative Provider Agreement

The following is a representative Provider Agreement without its mundane boilerplate provisions. It is not a copy of any specific insurer's provider contract to avoid the charge of disclosing secret proprietary information. However, it is an accurate representation of the Provider Agreements healthcare insurance companies use to ration the healthcare we are allowed to receive.

AGREEMENT

THIS PARTICIPATING PROVIDER AGREEMENT is made and entered into between **INSURER** and **HOSPITAL/DOCTOR/PROVIDER** to establish terms and conditions for the rendering and payment of services to Subscribers in accordance with insurance plans issued by **INSURER**.

NOW, THEREFORE, in consideration of the premises and mutual covenants contained herein and other good and valuable consideration, the receipt and sufficiency of which are hereby acknowledged, it is mutually agreed by and between the Parties as follows:

ARTICLE 1

DEFINITIONS

For the purpose of this Agreement, the following definitions shall apply:

1.1   CHARGES – The Hospital's/Doctor's/Provider's itemized listing of the rates it charges for patient services.

1.2   COVERED SERVICES – The services listed in a Subscriber's insurance benefit package AND rendered to the Subscriber.

1.3 NON-COVERED SERVICES – The services that are defined as NOT available services in the Subscriber's insurance Plan and benefit package *(typically limited to elective cosmetic surgery and experimental treatments).*

1.4 NETWORK – The participating providers with which Insurer, its affiliates, contractors and subcontractors has contracted to furnish COVERED SERVICES under a subscriber benefit package issued by Insurer.

1.5 ENROLLEE – A subscriber who is eligible to receive COVERED SERVICES under an insurance Plan and benefit package issued by Insurer.

1.6 SUBSCRIBER – An enrolled and eligible individual, or dependents, who has satisfied the criteria for benefits under an insurance Plan provided and administered by Insurer.

1.7 EMERGENCY – A sudden onset of acute medical or psychiatric symptoms of sufficient severity, that in the absence of immediate medical attention, could result in: 1.) Permanent injury to the subscriber, or 2.) Cause other serious medical or psychological consequences.

1.8 EMERGENCY CARE – Medically necessary care and services and supplies provided to a subscriber in an emergency.

1.9 MEDICALLY NECESSARY or APPROPRIATE CARE – The requirement that Covered Services are required, in the opinion of: (1.) the primary care physician, or the referred specialist, as applicable, consistent with Insurer's policies, coverage requirements and utilization guidelines; and (2.) Insurer, in order to diagnose and treat a subscriber, as applicable, and:

    a. Are provided in accordance with established standards and practices;

    b. Are required to improve the subscriber's health and health outcome; and

    c. Are as cost-effective as any available and ap proved alternative.

SECTION 2. PROVISION of COVERED SERVICES

2.1 Hospital/Doctor/Provider shall furnish Medically Necessary or Appropriate Services to eligible Subscribers in accordance with the terms and conditions of the Subscriber's insurance Plan and this Agreement.

2.2 Hospital/Doctor/Provider shall be solely responsible for the quality of Covered Services rendered to Subscriber. Hospital/Doctor further acknowledges that any action taken by Insurer pursuant to utilization management or cost containment **in no way absolves Hospital/Doctor/Provider of the responsibility to provide appropriate care to Subscriber** (Emphasis added by the author).

2.3 Covered Services shall be rendered a Subscriber by Hospital/Doctor/Provider without any advance deposit or other charge to Subscriber, except for copayments and deductible payments described in the Subscriber's insurance Plan.

2.4 Doctor/Hospital/Provider agrees to render Covered Services in accordance with: (a) all terms and conditions set forth in this Agreement, (b) all applicable laws and regulations, and (c) the same manner and timeliness as all other patients without regard to reimbursement (Emphasis added by the author).

SECTION 3. PAYMENT for SERVICES RENDERED

3.1 Hospital/Doctor/Provider shall submit claims for Covered Services no more than 90 days from the date the Covered Services are rendered.

3.2 Insurer shall pay Hospital/Doctor/Provider in accordance with the rates set herein for Medically Necessary and Appropriate Covered Services rendered Subscribers per the terms and conditions set forth in this Agreement.

3.3 Covered Services approved by Insurer and rendered by Hospital/Doctor/Provider shall be paid as provided herein, UNLESS: (a) excluded as a Non-Covered Service by a Subscribers insurance Plan and benefit package, (b) Insurer informs Hospital/Doctor that a given service is not a Covered Service, or (c) Insurer determines the service to be not Medically Necessary or Appropriate.

3.4 If all or any part of the Covered Services rendered a Subscriber by Hospital/Doctor/Provider was not ordered by a properly licensed health professional operating within the scope of that license, the Hospital/Doctor/Provider shall not bill or charge either Insurer or the Subscriber for that portion of the Covered Service.

3.5 Hospital/Doctor/Provider shall accept payments made by Insurer for Covered Services, including non-payment, as payment in full for all Covered Services rendered to a Subscriber and shall comply with the Employee Hold Harmless provision set forth below. **The Insurer's payment, including non-payment, shall therefore discharge all obligation of Subscriber for Covered Services** (Emphasis added by the author).

3.6 In the event Insurer makes an incorrect payment or an overpayment to Hospital/Doctor/ Provider, Hospital/Doctor/Provider agrees to refund or reimburse such amounts within five (5) business days. If Hospital/Doctor/Provider fails to refund or reimburse an overpayment, Hospital/Doctor/Provider hereby authorizes Insurer to withhold or offset future payments against amounts owed Hospital/Doctor/Provider.

SECTION 4. BILLING

4.1 Hospital/Doctor/Provider agree to submit bills to Insurer for Covered Services by the later of: (a) ninety days following the date Insurer issues billing approval to Hospital/Doctor/Provider or (2) ninety days following the last day of the calendar year in which the Subscriber was discharged from the hospital or ended treatment. If Hospital/Doctor/Provider fails to submit billing within this defined period, Insurer shall not be responsible for payment for those Covered Services and Hospital/Doctor/Provider shall not bill Subscriber for those Covered Services.

4.2   Insurer agrees to exercise its best efforts to pay appropriate claims for Covered Services within thirty (30) days of receipt of such claims.

SECTION 5. UTILIZATION REVIEW

5.1   All Covered Services rendered to Subscriber by Hospital/Doctor are subject to a medical and utilization review by Insurer or its designee.

5.2   Hospital/Doctor/Provider shall notify Insurer of all elective inpatient care to be rendered to a subscriber prior to admission or rendering such elective care.

5.3   Hospital/Doctor/Provider shall notify Insurer of all emergency admissions of Subscribers within one (1) business day of such admission.

5.4   Hospital/Doctor/Provider shall pre-certify all non-emergency admissions of Subscribers prior to admission by obtaining Insurer's approval of the Medical Necessity or Appropriateness of the admission and proposed length of stay.

5.5   Hospital/Doctor/Provider agrees Insurer shall not approve an inpatient admission until all necessary information is provided Insurer.

5.6   Where pre-certification is required but not performed, any and all services and days of care rendered prior to Insurer's pre-certification and approval shall not be billed or charged to Insurer or Subscriber.

5.7 Hospital/Doctor/Provider agrees Insurer shall review the Medical Necessity or Appropriateness of an inpatient admission or course of treatment on a daily basis and be free to find such admission or course of treatment not Medically Necessary or Appropriate.

5.8 **Whenever the Insurer's review of Medically Necessary or Appropriate determines a particular inpatient admission or course of treatment is not Medically Necessary or Appropriate, Hospital/Doctor shall not bill or charge Insurer or Subscriber for that denied stay or treatment** (Emphasis added by the author). Hospital/Doctor/Provider further agrees such reviews and denials can be retroactive and reverse earlier approvals by Insurer or Insurer's designee.

5.9 Whenever an admission or some portion of an admission is determined by Insurer to be not Medically Necessary or Appropriate or other requirements set forth herein are not met, the entire admission shall be denied and the Hospital/Doctor/Provider shall not bill or charge Insurer or Subscriber for any services associated with such denied stay or treatment.

5.10 Should Insurer determine a requested admission or course of treatment is not Medically Necessary or Appropriate and Hospital/Doctor/Provider nonetheless provides that admission or course of treatment, Hospital/Doctor/Provider shall not bill or charge Insurer or Subscriber for any related costs associated with that denied admission or treatment.

SECTION 6. EMPLOYEE HOLD HARMLESS

6.1 Hospital/Doctor/Provider agrees that in no event, including but not limited to non-payment by Insurer, Insurer's insolvency or breach of this Agreement, shall Hospital/Doctor/Provider, one of its subcontractors, or any of its employees or independent contractors bill, charge, collect a deposit from, seek compensation, remuneration or reimbursement from, or have any recourse against a Subscriber, or persons other than Insurer acting on behalf for services provided pursuant to this Agreement. This provision shall not prohibit the collection of coinsurance, copayments or charges for non-Covered Services. Hospital/Doctor/Provider further agrees that (1) this provision shall survive the termination of this Agreement regardless of the cause giving rise to the termination and shall be construed to be for the benefit of the Subscriber, and that (2) this provision supersedes any oral or written contrary agreement now existing or hereinafter entered into between Hospital/Doctor/Provider and Subscriber or persons acting on their behalf.

SECTION 7. CONFIDENTIALITY AND DISCLOSURE

7.1 Hospital/Doctor/Provider agree not to disclose any information pertaining to business conducted by Insurer, including, but not limited to the payments for Covered Services. Hospital/Doctor/Provider further agrees that all such information shall be considered confidential and proprietary and unless required by law, shall not be disclosed, except as otherwise approved by written consent of Insurer.

7.2 Hospital/Doctor/Provider specifically acknowledge and agree that a breach of the foregoing provisions will cause Insurer irreparable harm and that the remedy at law for any such breach will be inadequate and that Insurer, in addition to any other relief available to it, shall be entitled to equitable relief and temporary and permanent injunctive relief without the necessity of proving actual damages or posting any bond whatsoever.

SECTION 8. INDEMNIFICATION

8.1.1 Hospital/Doctor/Provider agrees to indemnify and hold harmless Insurer from any suit, cost, claim or expense, including, but not limited to, the cost of defense incurred by Insurer as a result of negligent actions or breach of this Agreement by Hospital/Doctor/Provider or their employees, contractors or subcontractors in connection with rendering Covered Services pursuant to this Agreement.

SECTION 9. TERM

9.1 This Agreement shall commence as of the date hereof and shall continue for three (3) years, and thereafter shall automatically renew for successive terms of one (1) year. Notwithstanding the foregoing, this Agreement shall not be effective until approved by State Department of Insurance/Health.

SECTION 10. TERMINATION

10.1 Either party may terminate this Agreement by providing the other party with not less than 60 days prior written notice.

10.2 Insurer may immediately terminate this Agreement if, in its sole opinion, Hospital/Doctor/ Provider fails to comply with any Insurer Policies or Procedures and such failure would reasonably have a material adverse effect on Insurer.

10.3 Insurer may immediately terminate this Agreement if, in its sole opinion, Hospital/Doctor/ Provider are in breach of any portion of this Agreement and failed to cure such Breach within 30 days of written notification by insurer.

10.4 In the event Hospital/Doctor/Provider is providing services to a Subscriber as of the date of termination of this Agreement, Hospital/Doctor/Provider shall continue to furnish those services and facilities contemplated to that Subscriber and all other Subscribers who were receiving such services on the date of termination. Hospital's/Doctor's/Provider's right to receive reimbursement for such Covered Services shall continue to be governed by the applicable terms of this Agreement. This provision shall survive the termination of this Agreement for any reason.

SECTION 11. APPEAL OF UTILIZATION REVIEW DETERMINATIONS

11.1 Hospital/Doctor/Provider has the right to appeal an adverse determination by Insurer or its designee on the Medical Necessity or Appropriateness of any requested inpatient admission, length of stay or course of treatment.

11.2 **Hospital/Doctor/Provider agree to comply with Insurer's policies, procedures and all final determinations of appropriate care and coverage** (Emphasis added by the author).

11.3 **Hospital/Doctor/Provider agrees decisions by the Insurer's Appeals Panel shall be final, binding and non-appealable for all parties** (Emphasis added by the author).

IN WITNESS WHEREOF, the undersigned have executed this Agreement on the date set forth below.

INSURANCE COMPANY   HOSPITAL/DOCTOR/PROVIDER

By: _____   By:_____

Appendix 6

NAIC's Suggested Enrollee Hold Harmless Language

The requirement of Subsection B shall be met by including a provision substantially similar to the following:

Provider agrees that in event, including but not limited to, nonpayment by health maintenance organization or intermediary organization, insolvency of the health maintenance organization or intermediary organization, or breach of this agreement shall the provider bill, charge, collect a deposit from, seek compensation, remuneration or reimbursement from, or have any recourse against a covered person or a person (other than the health maintenance organization or intermediary organization) acting on behalf of the covered person for covered services provided pursuant to this agreement. This agreement does not prohibit the provider from collecting coinsurance, deductibles, copayments or services in excess of limits as specifically provided in the evidence of coverage, or fees for uncovered services delivered on a fee-for-service basis to covered persons.

Any bill sent to a covered person shall include the following:

> Notice: You are not responsible for any
> amount owed by your insurer.

Please note of the last line above! For while NAIC's recommended language includes a recommendation that *"You are not responsible for any amount owed by your insurer,"* be included in every bill sent to an insured patient, you will not find the statement in any bill you and I ever get from an in-network provider. This says a ton about the healthcare insurance industry's willingness to be honest in its billing system.

Appendix 7

Pennsylvania's Enrollee Hold Harmless Clause

Hospital/Doctor/Provider agrees that in no event, including but not limited to non-payment by Insurance Company, Insurance Company's insolvency or breach of this agreement, shall Hospital, one of its subcontractors, or any of its employees or independent contractors bill, charge, collect a deposit from, seek compensation, remuneration or reimbursement from, or have any recourse against a Subscriber or persons other than the insurance company acting on behalf of Subscriber for Covered Services provided pursuant to this Agreement. This provision shall not prohibit the collection of coinsurance, co-payments or charges for Non-Covered Services. Hospital/Doctor/Provider further agrees that (1) this provision shall survive the termination of this Agreement regardless of the cause giving rise to termination and shall be construed to be for the benefit of the Subscribers, and that (2) this provision supersedes any oral or written contrary agreement now existing or hereafter entered into between Hospital/Doctor/Provider and Subscribers or persons acting on their behalf. Hospital/Doctor/ Hospital may not change, amend or waive this provision without prior written consent of the Insurance Company. Any attempt to change, amend or waive this provision are void.

Appendix 8

Advanced Beneficiary Notice
of Noncoverage (ABN)

Medicare Notification of Possible Noncoverage

A. Notifier:
B. Patient Name: C. Identification Number:

Advance Beneficiary Notice of Non-coverage
(ABN)

NOTE: If Medicare doesn't pay for D._____below, you may have to pay.
Medicare does not pay for everything, even some care that you or your health care provider have
good reason to think you need. We expect Medicare may not pay for the **D.**_____below.

D.	E. Reason Medicare May Not Pay:	F. Estimated Cost

WHAT YOU NEED TO DO NOW:
- Read this notice, so you can make an informed decision about your care.
- Ask us any questions that you may have after you finish reading.
- Choose an option below about whether to receive the **D.**_____listed above.

Note: If you choose Option 1 or 2, we may help you to use any other insurance that you
   might have, but Medicare cannot require us to do this.

G. OPTIONS: Check only one box. We cannot choose a box for you.

☐ **OPTION 1.** I want the **D.**_____listed above. You may ask to be paid now, but I
also want Medicare billed for an official decision on payment, which is sent to me on a Medicare
Summary Notice (MSN). I understand that if Medicare doesn't pay, I am responsible for
payment, but I can appeal to Medicare by following the directions on the MSN. If Medicare
does pay, you will refund any payments I made to you, less co-pays or deductibles.
☐ **OPTION 2.** I want the **D.**_____listed above, but do not bill Medicare. You may
ask to be paid now as I am responsible for payment. I cannot appeal if Medicare is not billed.
☐ **OPTION 3.** I don't want the **D.**_____listed above. I understand with this choice I
am **not** responsible for payment, and I cannot appeal to see if Medicare would pay.

H. Additional Information:

This notice gives our opinion, not an official Medicare decision. If you have other questions on this
notice or Medicare billing, call **1-800-MEDICARE** (1-800-633-4227/TTY: 1-877-486-2048).
Signing below means that you have received and understand this notice. You may ask to receive a copy.

I. Signature:	J. Date:

**You have the right to get Medicare information in an accessible format, like large print, Braille, or audio. You
also have the right to file a complaint if you feel you've been discriminated against. Visit Medicare.gov/about-
us/accessibility-nondiscrimination-notice.**

According to the Paperwork Reduction Act of 1995, no persons are required to respond to a collection of information unless it displays a valid OMB control number.
The valid OMB control number for this information collection is 0938-0566. The time required to complete this information collection is estimated to average 7 minutes
per response, including the time to review instructions, search existing data resources, gather the data needed, and complete and review the information collection. If
you have comments concerning the accuracy of the time estimate or suggestions for improving this form, please write to: CMS, 7500 Security Boulevard, Attn: PRA
Reports Clearance Officer, Baltimore, Maryland 21244-1850.

Form CMS-R-131 (Exp. XX/XX/XXXX)   Form Approved OMB No. 0938-0566

Appendix 9

A Letter to Our Insurance Company

Summarizing 67 Pages of Hidden Changes to the Plan the Author's Business Supplies its Employees

Dear Insurance Company:

The following are the points of concern in the 67-pages of terms and conditions that you claim are to be added to the plan we supposedly signed and finalized 2 weeks ago.

1.) In this Master Agreement we are to be bound by the insurer's Provider Agreements with the insurer's in-network providers of healthcare services:

Yet:

- These are Provider Agreements we have not been allowed to see.

- We are to accept full responsibility and liability for the delivery of coverage and care under these Provider Agreements.

- We are to allow our employees to be denied the third party rights that are specifically established by these Provider Agreements.

- We are barred from recovering any and all overpayments to in-network providers.

- And, the insurer is to have the final say in determining when coverage is appropriate under these Provider Agreements, while our business is to bear total responsibility and liability for these decisions.

2.) The Master Agreement also requires that we agree to "delegate" the insurer as the Plan's "Fiduciary" for the purpose of determining our employee's entitlement to plan benefits and coverage, and that the insurer's decisions on claims is final.

Yet:

- While, the Master Agreement makes it clear the insurer gets the final say on what qualifies as a covered benefit, our business is assigned the responsibility and liability for any fallout from the insurer's decisions.

3.) The Master Agreement states that the insurer does not render medical services, and that the insurer's in-network providers are solely responsible for the healthcare they deliver to Plan participants under the terms established by the insurer's Provider Agreements. The Master Agreement further states that the insurer is not responsible for any healthcare rendered under the Plan and its Provider Agreements.

Yet:

- The insurer is to be free to use "value-based contracting" with its in-network Providers to assure there are financial incentives impacting the medical decision-making of the insurer's in-network doctors. Simply put, the Master Agreement demands the freedom to ensure the determination of Medically Necessary Care is TEMPERED by cost, but accepts NO insurer responsibility or liability for the TEMPERING.

Respectfully,

My hope is that it will not come as a surprise that my wife and I: 1.) Got absolutely no response to the above letter, and 2.) Refused to accept the changes. And, we got zero response to our refusing the changes.

www.ingramcontent.com/pod-product-compliance
Lightning Source LLC
Chambersburg PA
CBHW042116190326
41519CB00030B/7518